Non-verbal Reasoning

Assessment Papers

10–11+ years

Book 1

OXFORD

UNIVERSITY PRESS

OXFORD
UNIVERSITY PRESS

Great Clarendon Street, Oxford, OX2 6DP, United Kingdom

Oxford University Press is a department of the University of Oxford.
It furthers the University's objective of excellence in research,
scholarship, and education by publishing worldwide. Oxford is
a registered trade mark of Oxford University Press in the UK and in
certain other countries

British Library Cataloguing in Publication Data
Data available

978-0-19-277643-3

10 9 8 7 6 5 4 3 2 1

Paper used in the production of this book is a natural, recyclable
product made from wood grown in sustainable forests.
The manufacturing process conforms to the environmental
regulations of the country of origin.

Printed in China

Acknowledgements

The publishers would like to thank the following for permissions to
use copyright material:

Page make-up: OKS Prepress, India
Illustrations: Bede Illustration
Cover illustrations: Lo Cole

Although we have made every effort to trace and contact all
copyright holders before publication this has not been possible in all
cases. If notified, the publisher will rectify any errors or omissions at
the earliest opportunity.

The publisher would like to thank Michellejoy Hughes for assisting with
the compilation of the expanded answers.

Links to third party websites are provided by Oxford in good faith
and for information only. Oxford disclaims any responsibility for
the materials contained in any third party website referenced in
this work.

Before you get started

What is Bond?

This book is part of the Bond Assessment Papers series for non-verbal reasoning, which provides a **thorough and progressive course in non-verbal reasoning** from ages six to twelve. It builds up reasoning skills from book to book over the course of the series.

Bond's non-verbal reasoning resources are ideal preparation for the 11+ and other secondary school selection exams.

How does the scope of this book match real exam content?

Non-verbal Reasoning 10–11+ years *Book 1* and *Book 2* are the core Bond 11+ books. Each paper is **pitched at the level of a typical 11+ exam** and practises a wide range of questions drawn from the four distinct groups of non-verbal reasoning question types: identifying shapes, missing shapes, rotating shapes, coded shapes and logic. The papers are fully in line with 11+ and other selective exams for this age group but are designed to practise **a wider variety of skills and question types** than most other practice papers so that children are always challenged to think – and don't get bored repeating the same question type again and again. We believe that variety is the key to effective learning. It helps children 'think on their feet' and cope with the unexpected: it is surprising how often children come out of non-verbal reasoning exams having met question types they have not seen before.

What does the book contain?

- **6 papers** – each one contains 60 questions.

- **Tutorial links throughout** – 📖 – this icon appears in the margin next to the questions. It indicates links to the relevant section in *How to do 11+ Non-verbal Reasoning*, our invaluable subject guide that offers explanations and practice for all core question types.

- **Scoring devices** – there are score boxes at the end of each paper and a Progress Chart on page 64. The chart is a visual and motivating way for children to see how they are doing. It also turns the score into a percentage that can help decide what to do next.

- **Next Steps Planner** – advice on what to do after finishing the papers can be found on the inside back cover.

- **Answers** – located in an easily-removed central pull-out section.

How can you use this book?

One of the great strengths of Bond Assessment Papers is their flexibility. They can be used at home, in school and by tutors to:

- set **timed formal practice** tests – allow about 45 minutes per paper in line with standard 11+ demands. Reduce the suggested time limit by five minutes to practise working at speed.

- provide **bite-sized chunks** for regular practice

- **highlight strengths and weaknesses** in the core skills

- identify **individual needs**

- set **homework**

- follow **a complete 11+ preparation strategy** alongside *The Parents' Guide to the 11+* (see below).

It is best to start at the beginning and work though the papers in order. If you are using the book as part of a careful run-in to the 11+, we suggest that you also have two other essential Bond resources close at hand:

How to do 11+ Non-verbal Reasoning: the subject guide that explains all the question types practised in this book. Use the cross-reference icons to find the relevant sections.

The Parents' Guide to the 11+: the step-by-step guide to the whole 11+ experience. It clearly explains the 11+ process, provides guidance on how to assess children, helps you to set complete action plans for practice and explains how you can use the *Non-verbal Reasoning 10–11+ years Book 1* and *Book 2* as part of a strategic run-in to the exam.

See the inside front cover for more details of these books.

What does your child's score mean and how can you improve it?

It is unfortunately impossible to guarantee that a child will pass the 11+ exam if they achieve a certain score on any practice book or paper. Success on the day depends on a host of factors, including the scores of the other children sitting the test. However, we can give some guidance on what a score indicates and how to improve it.

If children colour in the Progress Chart on page 64, this will give an idea of present performance in percentage terms. The Next Steps Planner inside the back cover will help you to decide what to do next to help a child progress. It is always valuable to go over wrong answers with children. If they are having trouble with any particular question type, follow the tutorial links to *How to do 11+ Non-verbal Reasoning* for step-by-step explanations and further practice.

Don't forget the website ... !

Visit www.bond11plus.co.uk for lots of advice, information and suggestions on everything to do with Bond, the 11+ and helping children to do their best.

Paper 1

Which shape on the right goes best with the shapes on the left? Circle the letter.

Example

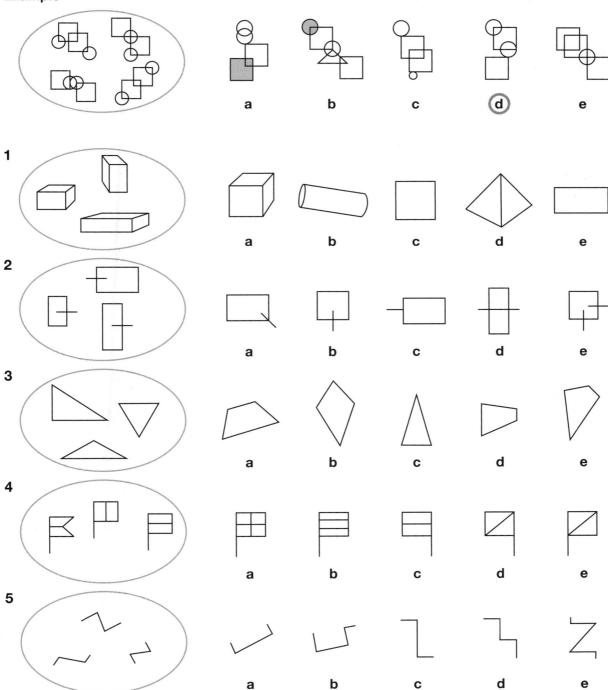

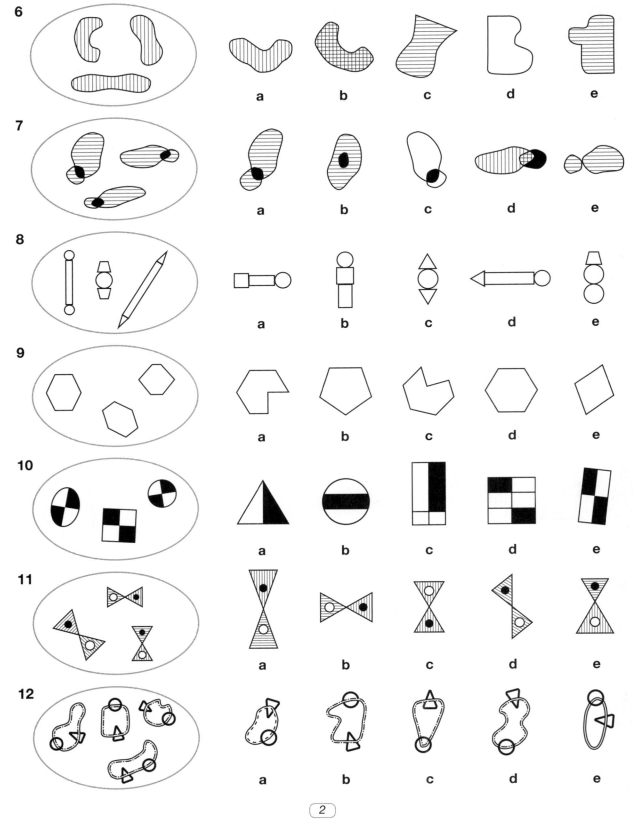

In which larger shape is the shape on the left hidden? Circle the letter.

Example

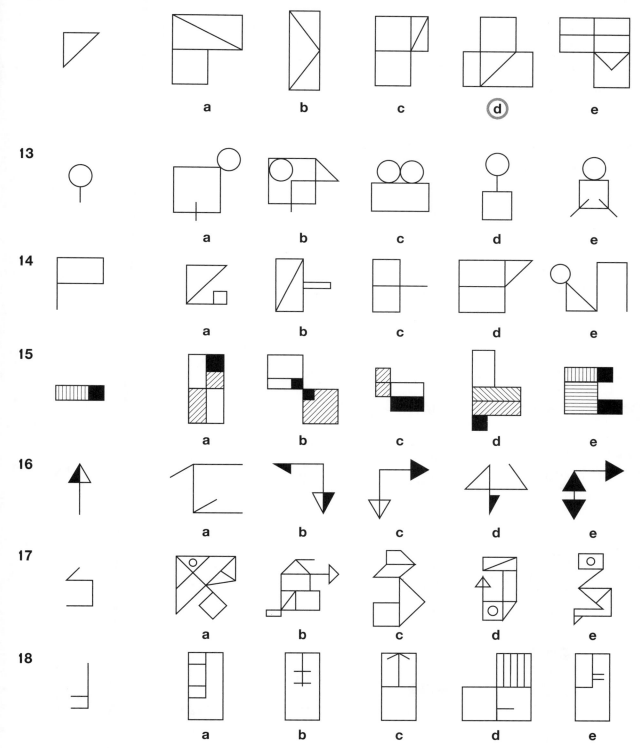

a   b   c   d   e

13

a   b   c   d   e

14

a   b   c   d   e

15

a   b   c   d   e

16

a   b   c   d   e

17

a   b   c   d   e

18

a   b   c   d   e

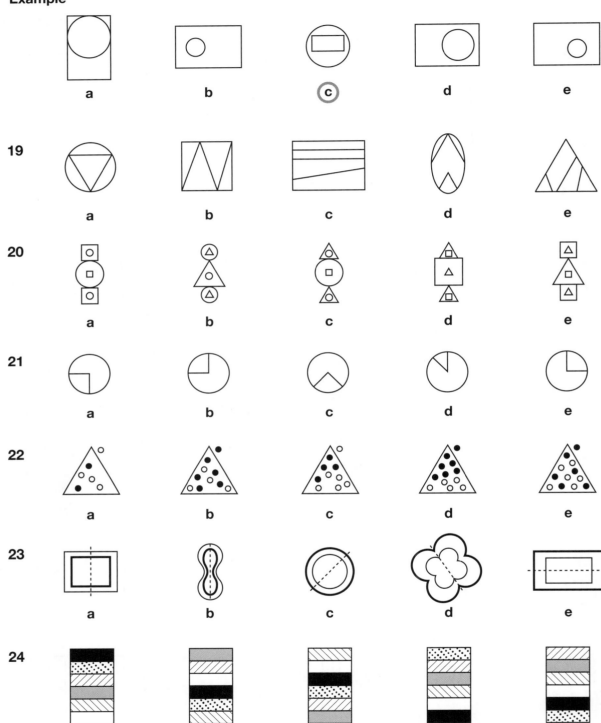

B 1 Which is the odd one out? Circle the letter.

Example

a   b   **c**   d   e

19   a   b   c   d   e

20   a   b   c   d   e

21   a   b   c   d   e

22   a   b   c   d   e

23   a   b   c   d   e

24   a   b   c   d   e

Which shape or pattern on the right completes the second pair in the same way as the first pair? Circle the letter.

Example

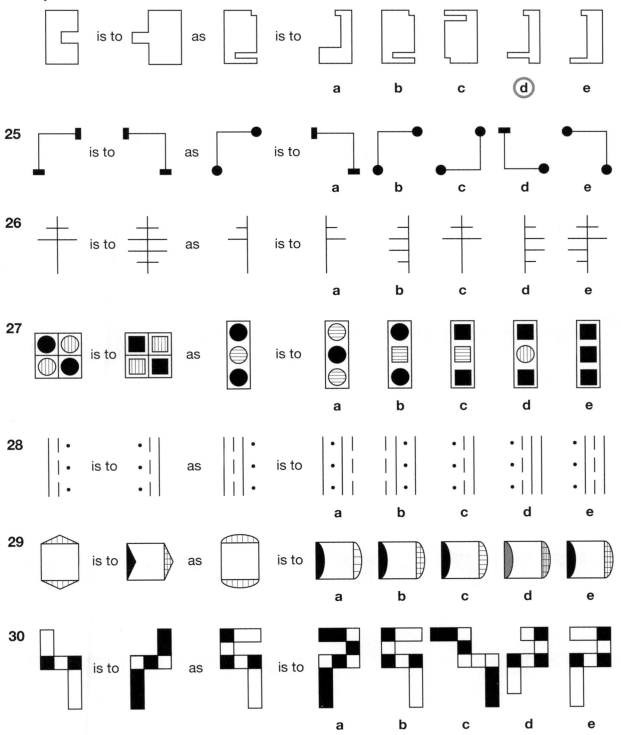

 **B 4** Which one comes next? Circle the letter.

Example

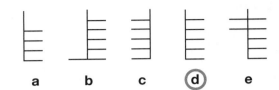

a   b   c   **(d)**   e

31

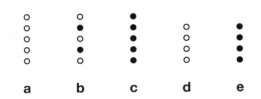

a   b   c   d   e

32

a   b   c   d   e

33

a   b   c   d   e

34

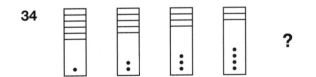 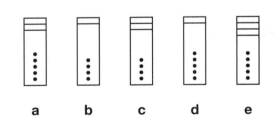

a   b   c   d   e

35

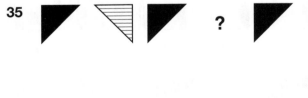 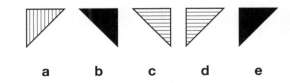

a   b   c   d   e

36

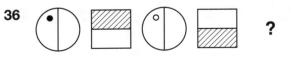 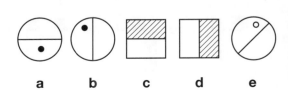

a   b   c   d   e

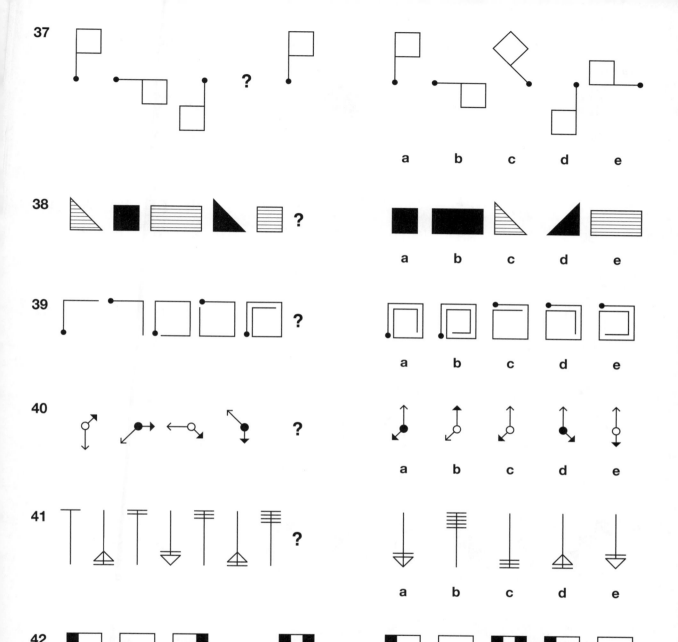

37

a   b   c   d   e

38

a   b   c   d   e

39

a   b   c   d   e

40

a   b   c   d   e

41

a   b   c   d   e

42

a   b   c   d   e

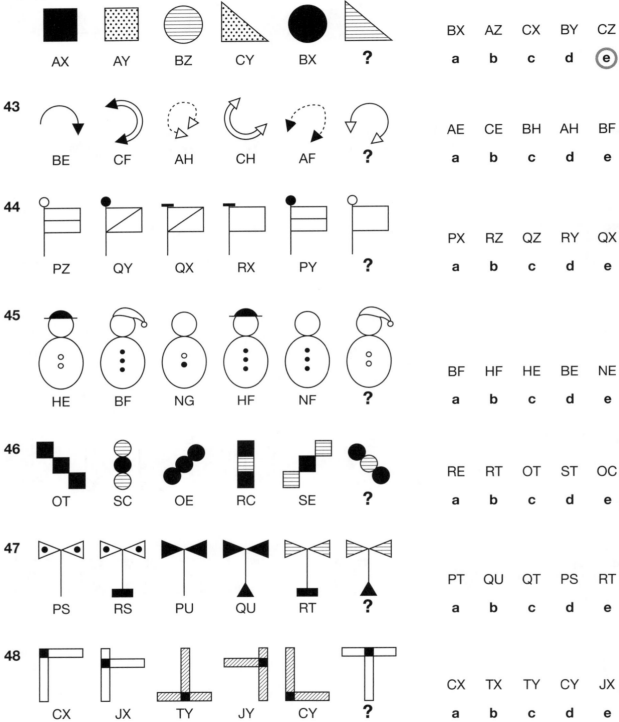

B 9 Which code matches the shape or pattern given at the end of each line? Circle the letter.

Example

AX AY BZ CY BX **?**   BX AZ CX BY CZ
                              a   b   c   d   (e)

43 BE CF AH CH AF **?**   AE CE BH AH BF
                                 a   b   c   d   e

44 PZ QY QX RX PY **?**   PX RZ QZ RY QX
                                 a   b   c   d   e

45 HE BF NG HF NF **?**   BF HF HE BE NE
                                 a   b   c   d   e

46 OT SC OE RC SE **?**   RE RT OT ST OC
                                 a   b   c   d   e

47 PS RS PU QU RT **?**   PT QU QT PS RT
                                 a   b   c   d   e

48 CX JX TY JY CY **?**   CX TX TY CY JX
                                 a   b   c   d   e

Which shape or pattern completes the larger square? Circle the letter.

Example

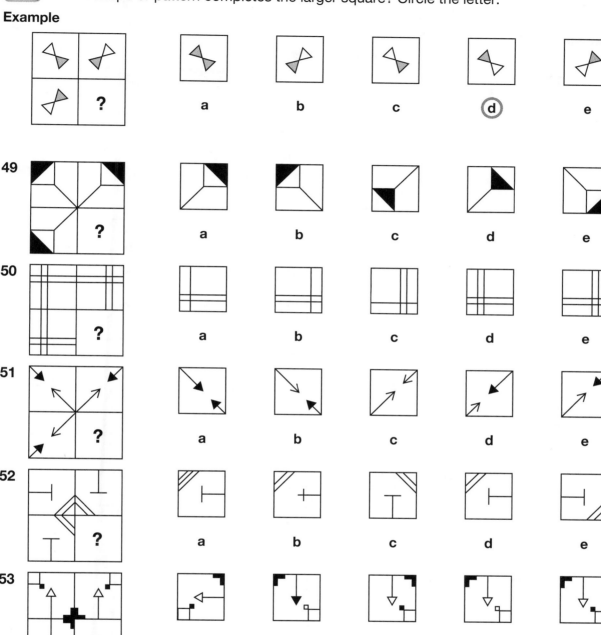

49 a b c d e

50 a b c d e

51 a b c d e

52 a b c d e

53 a b c d e

54 a b c d e

B 10 Which shape or pattern is made when the first two shapes or patterns are put together? Circle the letter.

Example

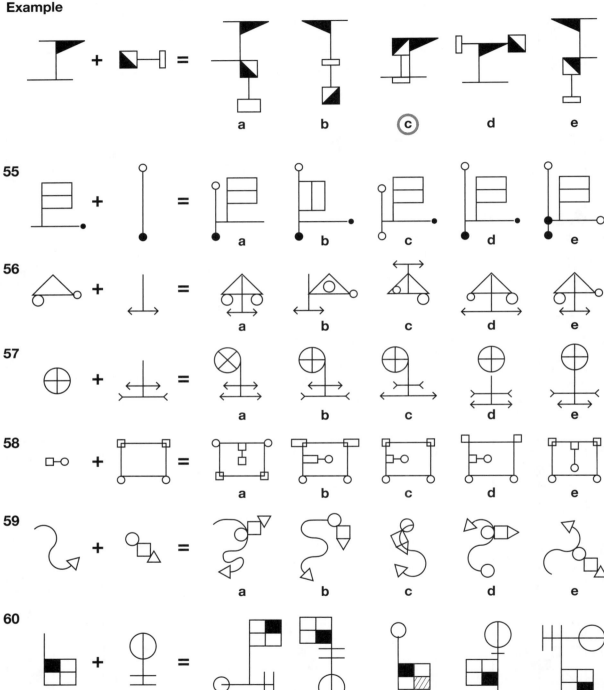

55

56

57

58

59

60

Paper 2

B 3 Which shape or pattern on the right completes the second pair in the same way as the first pair? Circle the letter.

Example

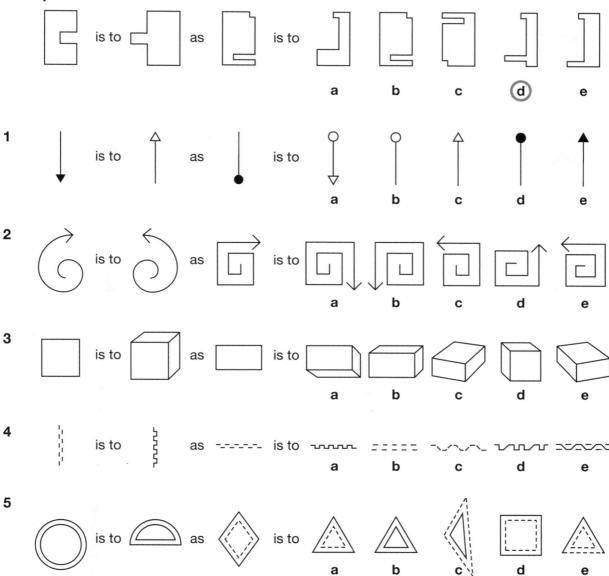

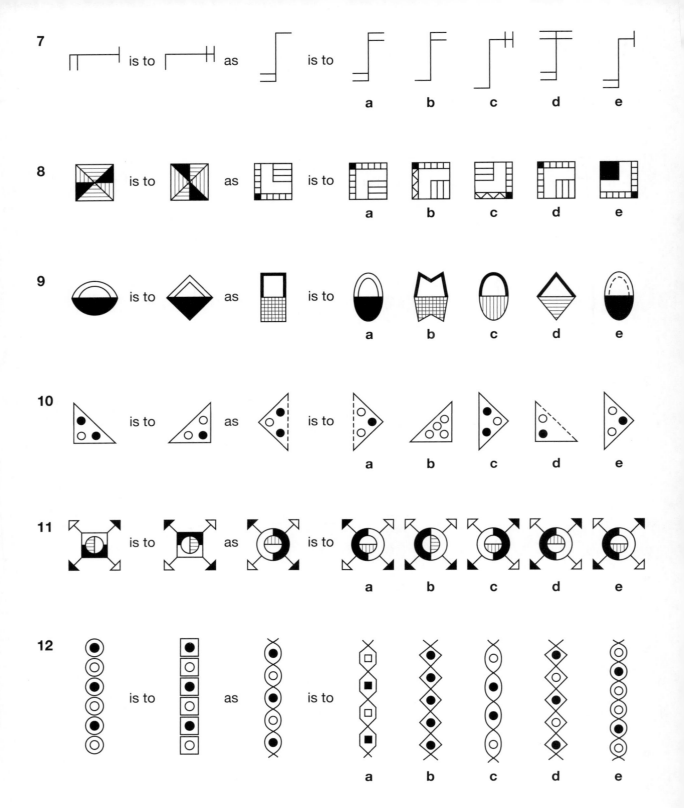

Which one comes next? Circle the letter.

Example

a   b   c   (d)   e

13

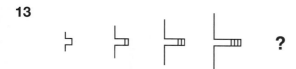

a   b   c   d   e

14

a   b   c   d   e

15

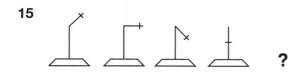

a   b   c   d   e

16

a   b   c   d   e

17

a   b   c   d   e

18

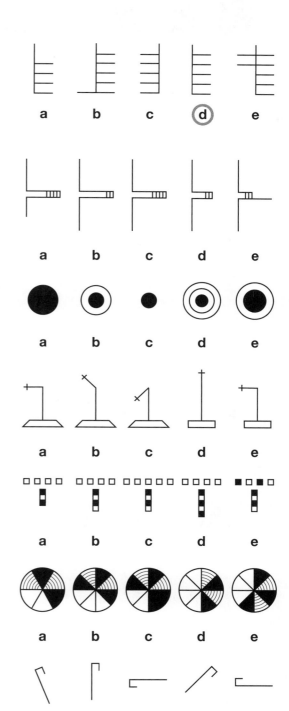

a   b   c   d   e

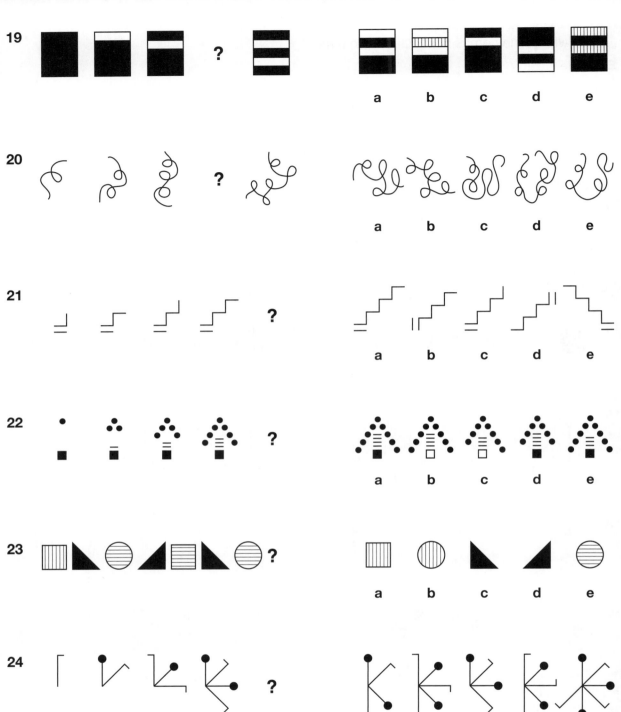

19

20

21

22

23

24

a b c d e

B 9 Which code matches the shape or pattern given at the end of each line? Circle the letter.

Example

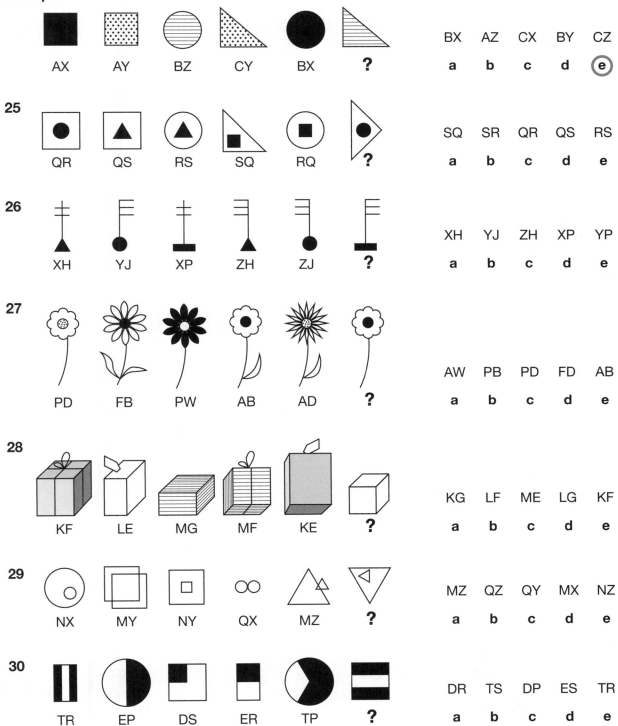

25	SQ	SR	QR	QS	RS
	a	b	c	d	e

26	XH	YJ	ZH	XP	YP
	a	b	c	d	e

27	AW	PB	PD	FD	AB
	a	b	c	d	e

28	KG	LF	ME	LG	KF
	a	b	c	d	e

29	MZ	QZ	QY	MX	NZ
	a	b	c	d	e

30	DR	TS	DP	ES	TR
	a	b	c	d	e

15

Which shape on the right goes best with the shapes on the left? Circle the letter.

Example

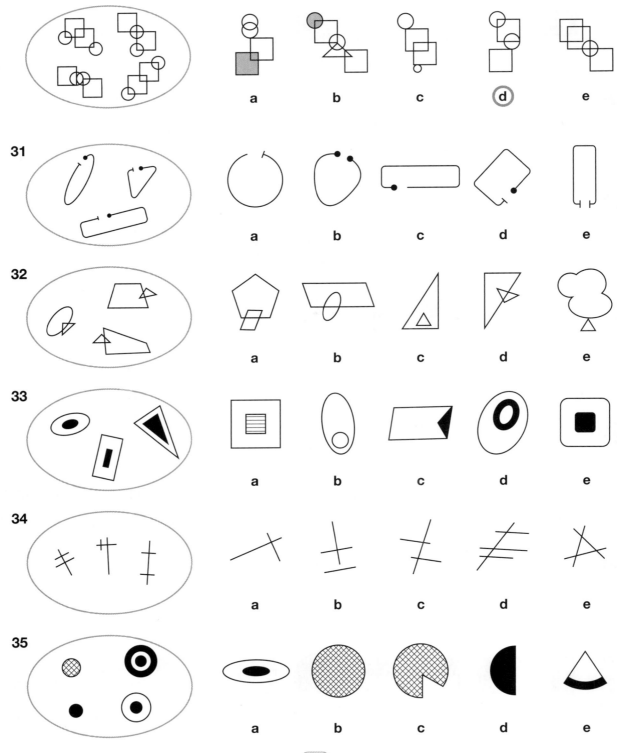

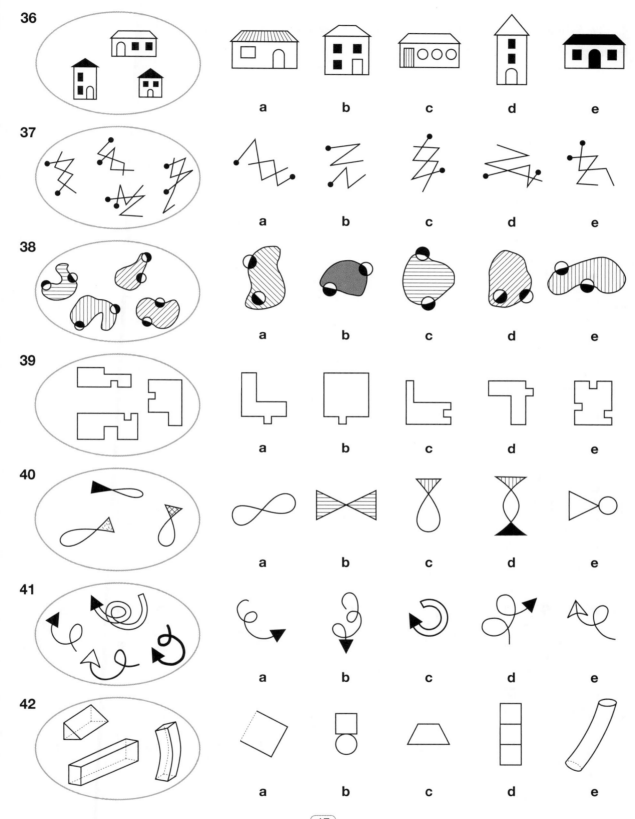

36

a   b   c   d   e

37

a   b   c   d   e

38

a   b   c   d   e

39

a   b   c   d   e

40

a   b   c   d   e

41

a   b   c   d   e

42

a   b   c   d   e

Which shape or pattern completes the larger square. Circle the letter.

Example

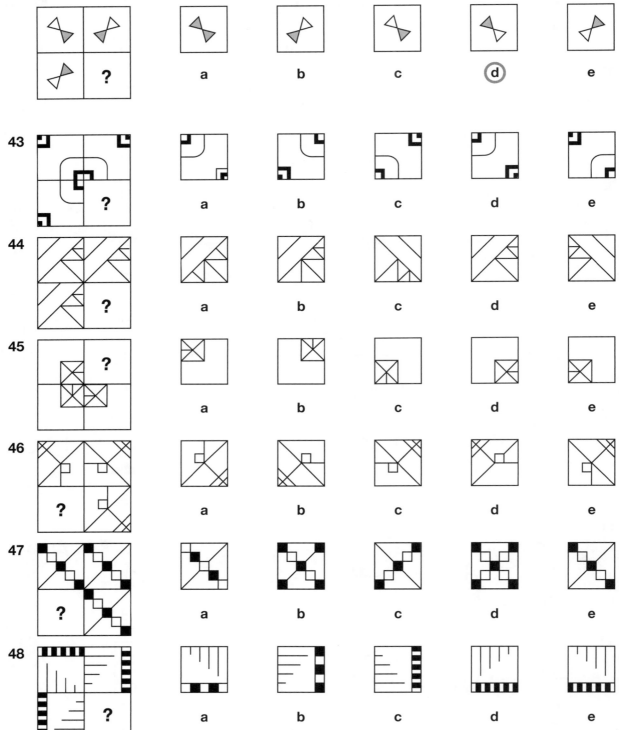

Which cube can be made from the given net? Circle the letter.

Example

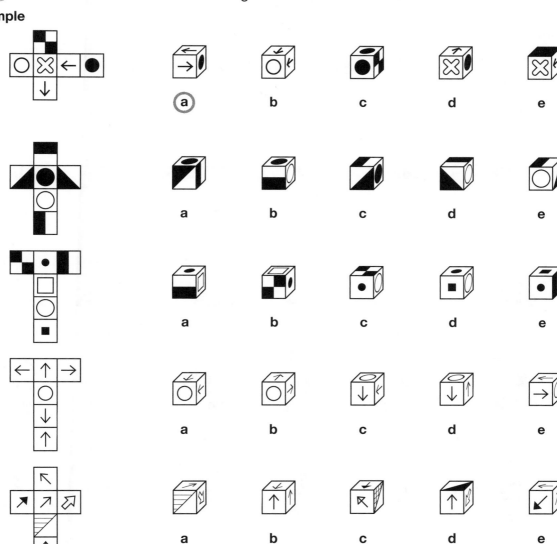

a   b   c   d   e

49

a   b   c   d   e

50

a   b   c   d   e

51

a   b   c   d   e

52

a   b   c   d   e

53

a   b   c   d   e

54

a   b   c   d   e

Which shape on the right is the reflection of the shape given on the left?
Circle the letter.

Example

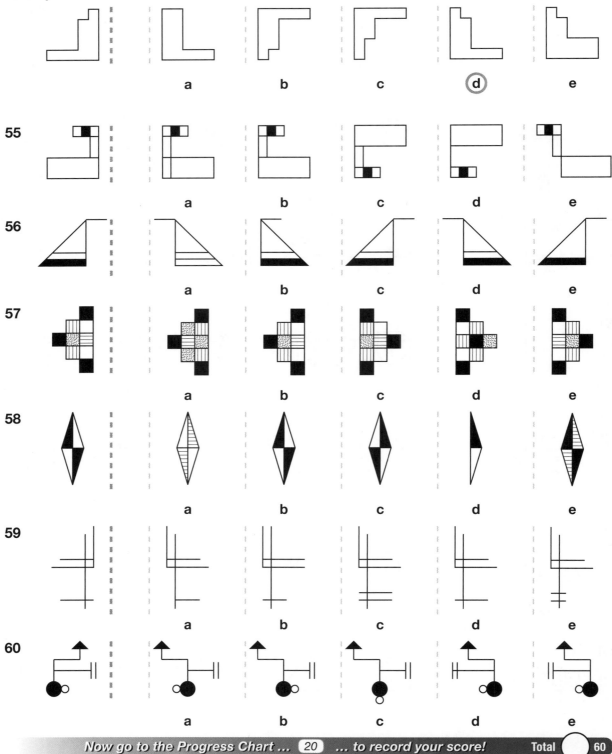

55

56

57

58

59

60

Paper 3

Which shape on the right goes best with the shapes on the left? Circle the letter.

Example

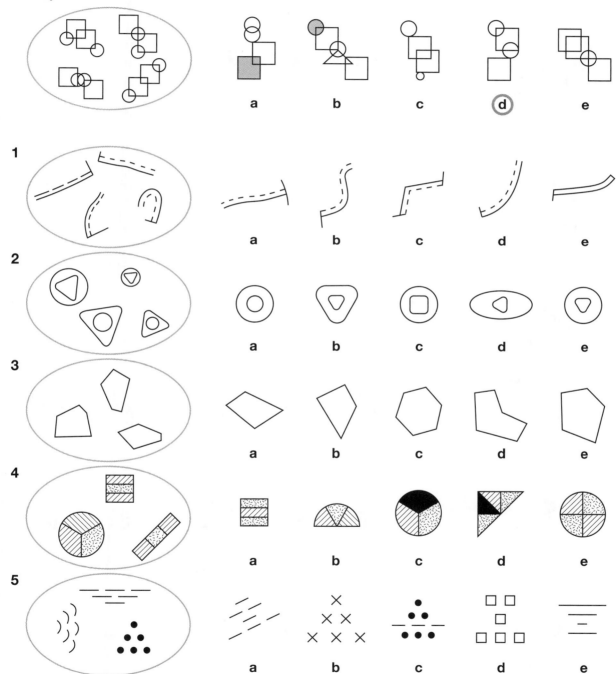

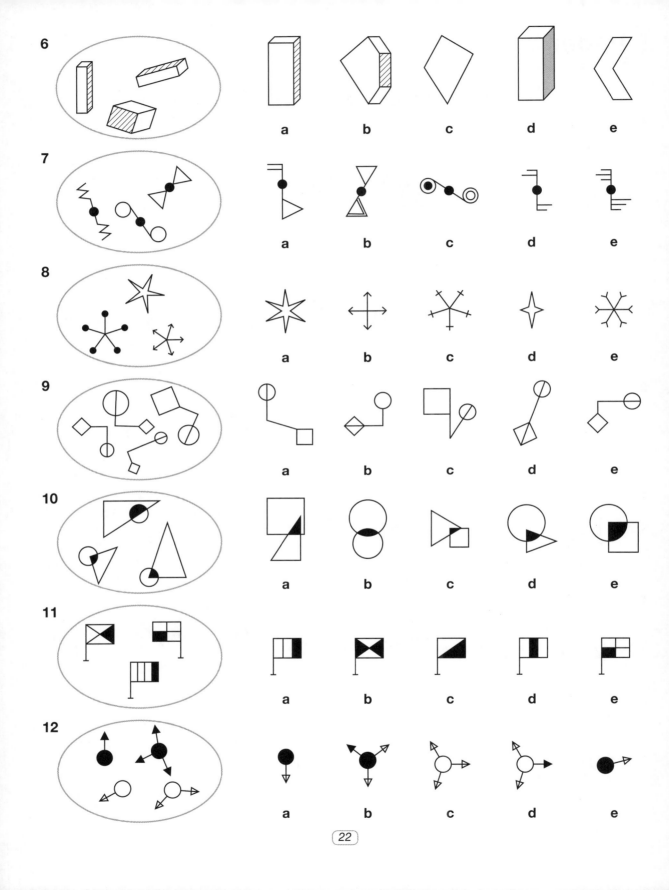

 Which one comes next? Circle the letter.

Example

 **?**

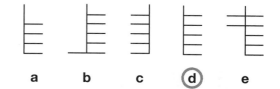

a   b   c   (d)   e

13  **?**

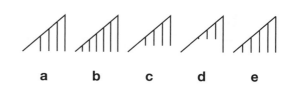

a   b   c   d   e

14

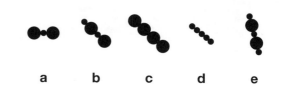

a   b   c   d   e

15

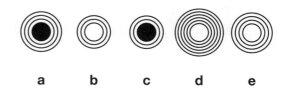

a   b   c   d   e

16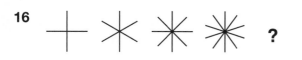

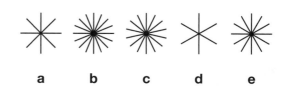

a   b   c   d   e

17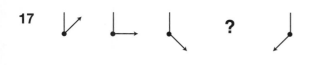

a   b   c   d   e

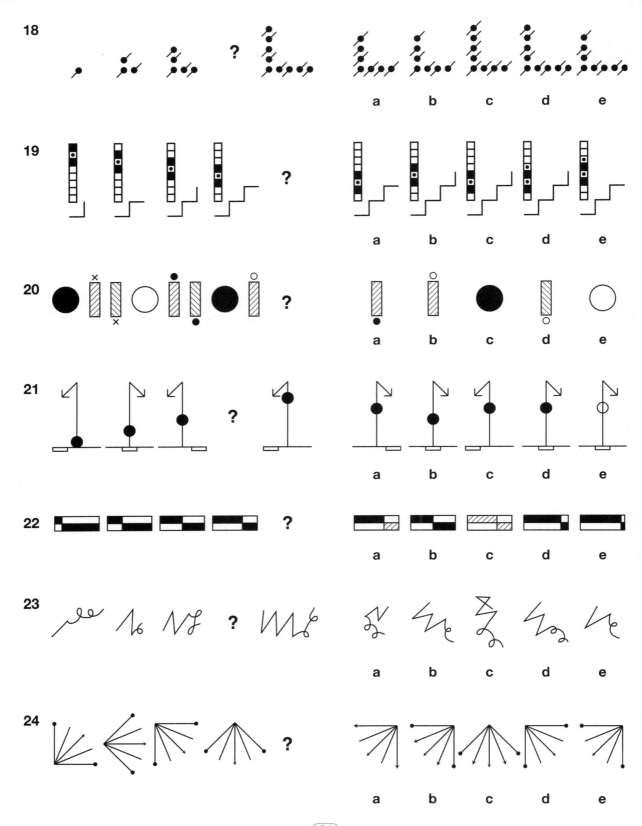

Which code matches the shape or pattern given at the end of each line.
Circle the letter.

Example

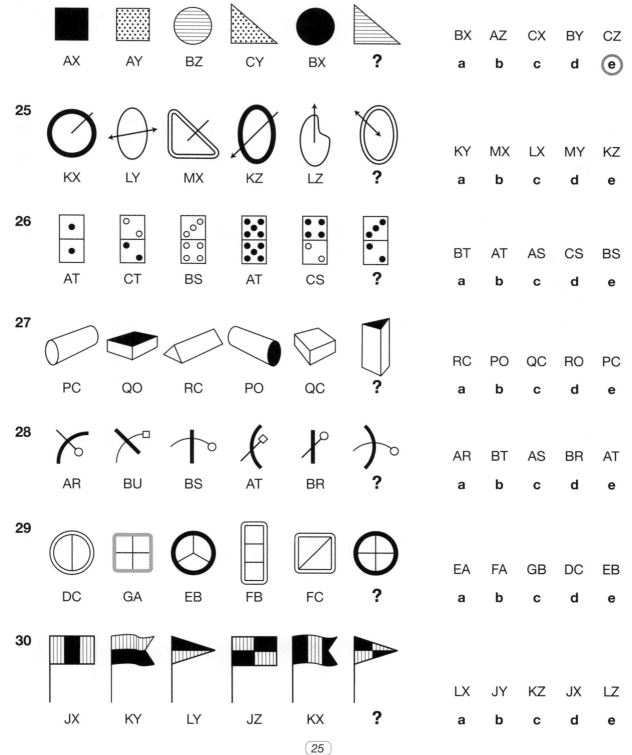

	BX	AZ	CX	BY	CZ
	a	b	c	d	(e)

25

	KY	MX	LX	MY	KZ
	a	b	c	d	e

26

	BT	AT	AS	CS	BS
	a	b	c	d	e

27

	RC	PO	QC	RO	PC
	a	b	c	d	e

28

	AR	BT	AS	BR	AT
	a	b	c	d	e

29

	EA	FA	GB	DC	EB
	a	b	c	d	e

30

	LX	JY	KZ	JX	LZ
	a	b	c	d	e

Which shape or pattern completes the larger square? Circle the letter.

Example

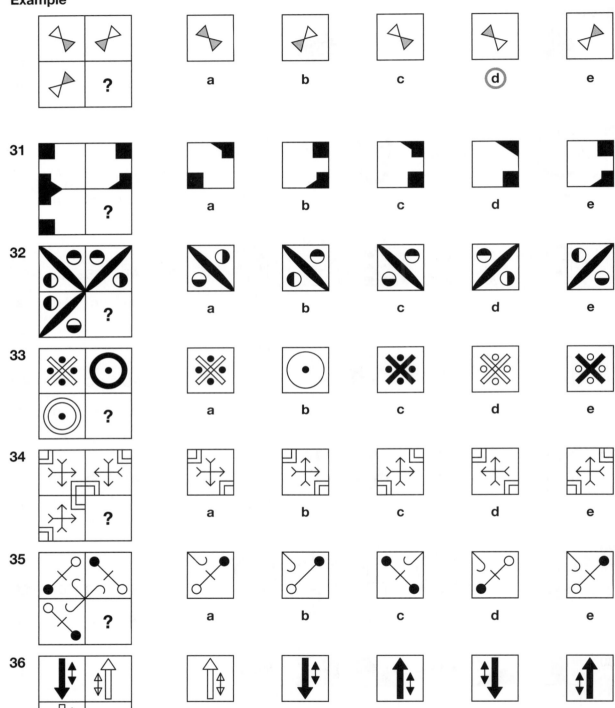

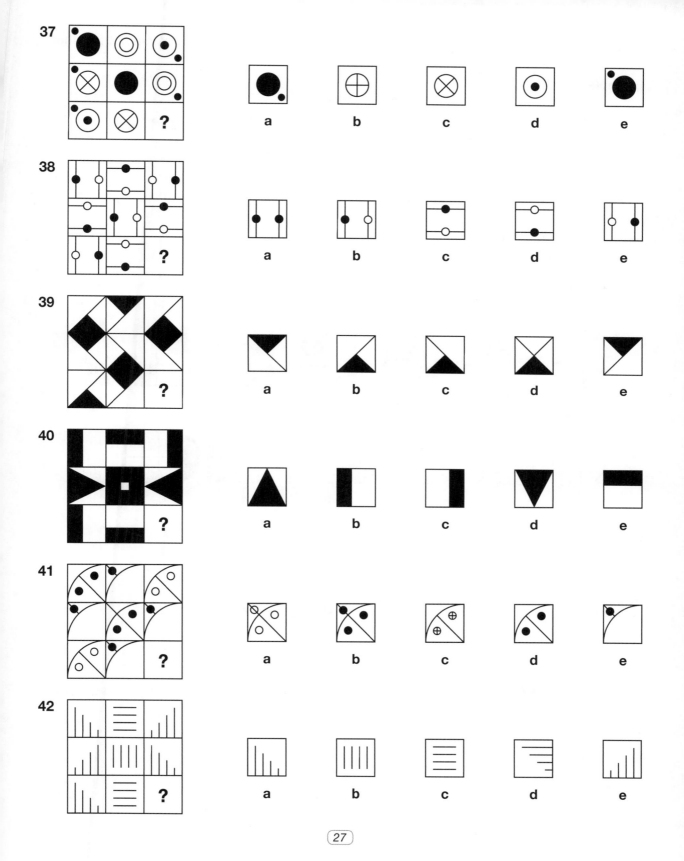

B 10 Which shape or pattern is made when the first two shapes or patterns are put together? Circle the letter.

Example

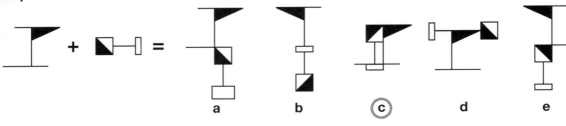

a   b   ⓒ   d   e

43

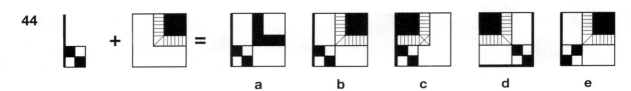

a   b   c   d   e

44

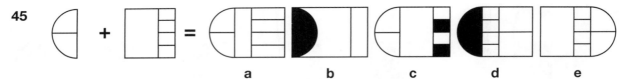

a   b   c   d   e

45

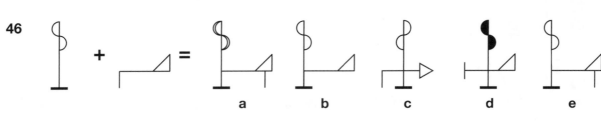

a   b   c   d   e

46

a   b   c   d   e

47

a   b   c   d   e

48

a   b   c   d   e

28

Which shape or pattern on the right completes the second pair in the same way as the first pair? Circle the letter.

Example

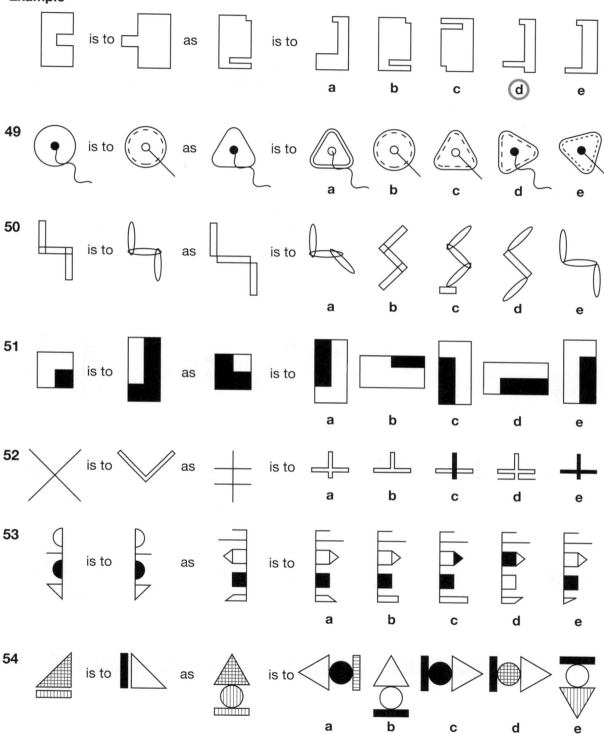

49

50

51

52

53

54

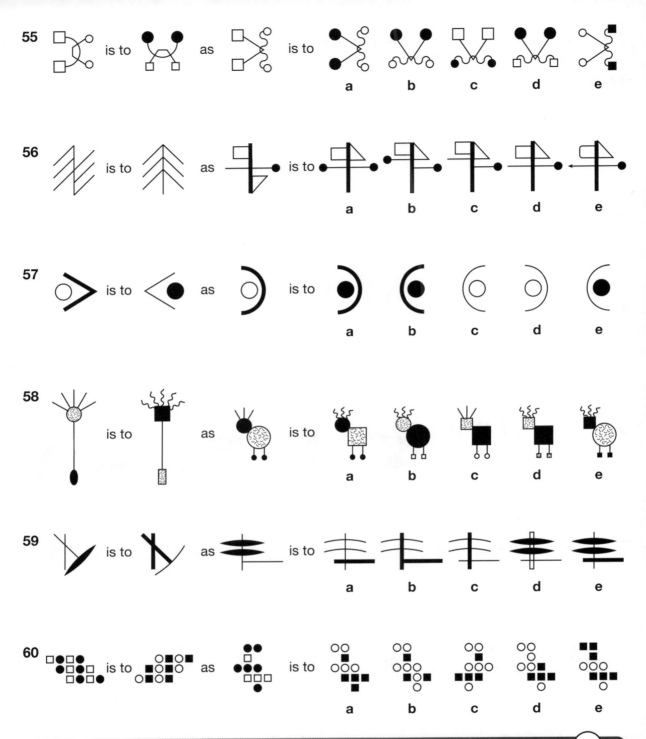

Now go to the Progress Chart to record your score!   Total   60

30

1 **a** All of the shapes are cuboids.

2 **b** All of the shapes have just one line placed half inside the shape and half outside the shape. The line does not cut through the shape, nor does it dissect a corner.

3 **c** All of the shapes are *triangles*.

4 **e** All of the flags are on the right of the pole. They are divided in half, either horizontally, vertically or diagonally.

5 **c** All of the shapes have only three lines and form the letter "z".

6 **a** All of the shapes are filled with vertical lines.

7 **a** All of the shapes are made from one large and one small shape, filled with horizontal lines and joined together with a black oval.

8 **c** All of the shapes are made up of three sections. The two end sections are the same shape. The middle section is different from the end sections.

9 **d** All of the shapes are hexagons, meaning that they have six sides.

10 **e** All of the shapes are divided into four equal sections. Half the sections are black and the other half are white, forming a chequered pattern.

11 **b** All of the shapes can be rotated so that the black circle is at the top. In this position, the black circles are on a background of horizontal lines. The white circles are on a background of vertical lines. The top and bottom of the bow are the same size.

12 **d** All of the shapes have a solid outer line and an inner broken line made up of alternating dots and dashes. The outer shape has a triangle behind it and a circle in front of it. The triangle points into the centre of the shape.

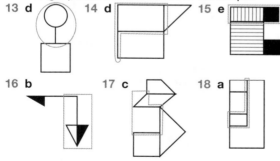

13 **d**   14 **d**   15 **e**

16 **b**   17 **c**   18 **a**

19 **d** All of the shapes apart from d have 3 lines inside the shape.

20 **c** All of the shapes have a top and bottom shape that are identical, with a different shape in the middle. In the centre of each middle shape there is a smaller shape, which is the same as the top and bottom shape. The odd one out is c

because the shape inside the middle circle should be a triangle rather than a square.

21 **d** All of the circles apart from d have one 90° segment inside.

22 **e** If a triangle has more black dots than white dots inside it, the dot outside the triangle is black. If there are more white dots inside, the outside dot is white. The only triangle that does not fit this pattern is e, which has more white dots inside but a black dot outside.

23 **b** All of the shapes apart from b have a dotted line through the centre which extends beyond the edges of the shape.

24 **b** The blocks appear in the same order in each shape, but in b the blocks with diagonal lines on them have swapped positions.

25 **e** The second shape is a vertical reflection of the first shape.

26 **b** The second shape has a horizontal reflection added to the first shape.

27 **c** The second shape has the circles replaced by squares.

28 **e** The second shape is a vertical reflection of the first shape.

29 **e** The second shape is rotated 90° clockwise. The highest shape is now on the right and the pattern has changed from vertical lines to a check pattern. The lowest shape is now on the left and is flipped along the horizontal line so that the shape is now inside the middle shape. The pattern of this shape has changed from vertical lines to black.

30 **a** The second shape is a vertical reflection of the first shape. The white blocks have become black and the black blocks have become white.

31 **c** The dots continue to increase in number. The dots alternate between black and white.

32 **d** There is one additional line added each time.

33 **d** The number of circles increases each time. The circles alternate between a solid line and a broken line.

34 **d** The dots continue to increase in number as the lines decrease in number.

35 **c** The triangles alternate between a black triangle with a right angle at the top left and a triangle with horizontal lines with the right angle at the top right.

36 **b** The shapes alternate between a circle and a square. The circles are divided by a vertical line and the small dot in the left half alternates between black and white.

37 **e** The flags rotate 90° clockwise around the black circle.

38 **b** The shapes form a repeating sequence of triangle, square, rectangle. The pattern inside the shapes alternates between horizontal lines and black.

EXPANDED ANSWERS

Bond Non-Verbal Reasoning Assessment Papers 10–11+ years Book 1

39 **d** The number of lines follows a pattern of 2 lines, 2 lines, 4 lines, 4 lines, 6 lines, 6 lines. The black circle alternates between bottom left and top left as the shape rotates clockwise 90°, then anticlockwise 90°.

40 **c** The entire shape rotates 45° clockwise. The circle at the centre alternates between white and black.

41 **e** The 'T' shapes have an increasing number of lines and alternate with the triangle pattern. The triangle pattern alternates between the triangle apex pointing upwards with the line extending through it, and the triangle apex pointing downwards with the line not extending through it. The base line alternates between being under the triangle pointing upwards and above the triangle pointing downwards.

42 **c** The number of black squares increases by one each time.

43 **c** The first letter represents the curve (A has a dashed line curve, B has a single line curve and C has a double line curve). The second letter represents the arrowheads (E has one black arrow, F has two black arrows and H has two white arrows).

44 **b** The first letter represents the internal flag pattern (P has a horizontal line, Q has a diagonal line and R has no internal line). The second letter represents the top left-hand shape (X has a black rectangle, Y has a black circle and Z has a white circle).

45 **d** The first letter represents the hat (B is a bobble hat, H is a black bowler hat and N has no hat at all). The second letter represents the buttons (E has two white buttons, F has three black buttons and G has one white and one black button).

46 **b** The first letter represents the shading (O has three black shapes, R has two black and one lined shape and S has one black and two lined shapes). The second letter represents the direction of the shapes (T is diagonal running top left to bottom right, C is a vertical stack and E is diagonal running bottom left to top right).

47 **c** The first letter represents the bottom shape (P has no shape at the bottom, R has a black rectangle and Q has a black triangle). The second letter represents the appearance of the bows (S has one black dot in each bow, U has two solid black bows and T has two striped bows).

48 **b** The first letter represents the way the two rectangles join (C is formed by two rectangles joined at the corners, J has a small section of one rectangle extending beyond the join and T has one rectangle divided into two by the other). The second letter represents the colour of the rectangles (X is white and Y has diagonal lines).

49–54 In all of the completed shapes, the bottom right missing square will be a diagonal reflection of the top left square.

49 **e**

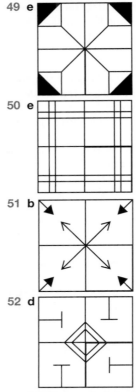

50 **e**

51 **b**

52 **d**

The T shape rotates 90° in a clockwise direction. The two lines at the centre are diagonal reflections of the two lines in the top left square.

53 **e**

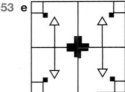

The bottom right missing square is a horizontal reflection of the top right square.

54 **c**

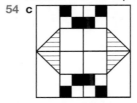

The bottom right missing square is a horizontal reflection of the top right square.

55 **d**

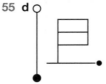

A2

The line with beads at either end is the correct length, with one bead at each end. In the other shape, the rectangles are horizontal and there is a small black bead at the end of the horizontal line.

56 e

The triangle shape has two circles that are the correct size and position. The second shape is placed beneath it, with the upright stalk passing through the triangle and touching its apex.

57 b

The circle shape appears at the top of the combined shape. The second shape has arrows pointing outwards on the short upper line, and arrows pointing inwards on the longer bottom line.

58 c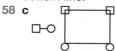

The first shape consists of a small square and a similar-sized circle, joined by a short line. The second shape has squares at two corners that overlap the corners of the rectangle, and circles sitting just outside the other two corners.

59 e

The first shape has been rotated 180°, but the shape of the curve is correct and there is a triangle at one end. In the second shape, the smaller shapes are oriented correctly, with the circle touching one corner of the square and the triangle touching the corner that is diagonally opposite.

60 b

The first shape has been rotated 180°, with the black segment in the correct position. The second shape has also been rotated 180°, then joined to the 'flagpole' of the first shape.

1 **b** The second shape has been rotated 180° and the black shape at the end has become a white version of the same shape.
2 **c** The second shape has been reflected in a vertical mirror line.
3 **b** The 2D shape has been turned into a 3D shape. The 3D shape is in the same position shown in the first pair.
4 **a** The lines have been joined up by adding lines at a 90° angle.
5 **a** The second shape is half of the first shape. The outer lines stays as a thin, black line and inner line stays as a broken line.
6 **c** The second shape has been reduced in size and reflected in a diagonal mirror line.
7 **b** The double vertical lines at one end of the first shape have been reduced to a single line, while the single vertical line at the other end has become a double line.
8 **d** The second shape has been rotated 90° clockwise.
9 **b** The second shape is a more angular version of the first shape. The pattern remains the same.
10 **a** The outer shape of the second shape is a vertical reflection of the outer shape of the first shape. The black dots on the inside have become white and the white dots have become black.
11 **e** The black and white elements of the first shape are opposite in the second shape, so the black parts become white and the white parts become black. The central circle has been rotated 180°.
12 **d** The outer circles have become squares. The inner circles stay the same shape, size and colour.
13 **c** The horizontal block grows longer and the number of lines on it increases. The top and bottom vertical lines increase in length.
14 **e** The circles form a sequence of a large black circle followed by a small white circle, then a medium black circle with a ring around it and finally a small black circle. The sequence then begins again.
15 **c** The angled part of the top line rotates clockwise 45°.
16 **b** The number of white squares in the top row increases by one. The vertical line of squares below it also increases by one, alternating between black and white.
17 **b** The black wedge moves one position clockwise each time and is replaced by another wedge. The pattern of the wedges alternates between black and lined.
18 **e** The shape rotates clockwise 45°.

EXPANDED ANSWERS

Bond Non-Verbal Reasoning Assessment Papers 10–11+ years Book 1

19 **a** The sequence begins with a completely black shape and then alternates between black and white rectangles that move downwards each time.

20 **a** The number of loops in the shape increases by one.

21 **c** The number of lines in the upper shape increases by one, with the lines angled to form a shape like a set of stairs. Each shape has a single horizontal line below it.

22 **a** The number of black circles increases by two, with the dots added at the bottom to form an arrowhead shape. The black square at the bottom remains the same, but the number of horizontal lines above it increases by one.

23 **d** Every second shape is a black triangle, and each time the triangle is reflected in a vertical mirror line.

24 **d** The hook shape rotates clockwise 45°. As it moves, it is replaced in the '12:00' position by another shape, which alternates between a stick with a black dot around it, and another hook. Each additional hook points the opposite way to the previous hook.

25 **b** The first letter represents the outer shape (Q is a square, R is a circle and S is a triangle). The second letter represents the inside shape (R is a circle, S is a triangle and Q is a square).

26 **e** The first letter represents the horizontal lines on top (X has 2 central lines, Y has 3 lines pointing to the right and Z has 3 lines pointing to the left). The second letter represents the bottom black shape (H is a triangle, J is a circle and P is a rectangle).

27 **b** The first letter represents the leaves (P has no leaves, F has two leaves and A has one leaf). The second letter represents the colour of the flower's centre (D is white with black dots, B is black and W is white)

28 **d** The first letter represents the colour of the box (K is grey, L is white and M has horizontal lines). The second letter represents the closure of each box (F has a tied bow, E has a gift tag and G has no visible closure).

29 **e** The first letter represents the position of the two shapes (N has a small shape inside a larger shape, M has one shape overlapping the other and Q has 2 shapes of identical size joined to each other). The second letter represents the shapes (X is a pair of circles, Y is a pair of squares and Z is a pair of triangles).

30 **b** The first letter represents the proportion of black to white in each pattern (T has two-thirds black to one-third white, E has equal amounts of black and white and D has one-quarter black to three-quarters white). The second letter represents the outer shape (R is a

rectangle, P is a circle and S is a square).

31 **d** All of the shapes have a small gap between the two ends. One end has a black circle and the other end forms a 'T' shape.

32 **d** All of the shapes have a small triangle that overlaps the large shape.

33 **e** All of the shapes have a black shape in the middle that has the same shape as the outer shape.

34 **c** All of the shapes have three lines, with two of them crossing the first at a 90° angle.

35 **b** All of the shapes are complete circles.

36 **d** All of the houses have two black windows and one white, arched door.

37 **c** All of the shapes have two zigzag lines, and each line has a black dot on one end. The crossing of the two zigzag lines forms two complete shapes.

38 **e** All of the shapes are filled with a pattern of lines. They have two circles that overlap the edges, and these circles have one black half facing inwards and one black half facing outwards.

39 **c** All of the shapes have one small notch taken out of the shape.

40 **c** All of the shapes are made from a rounded teardrop shape attached to a triangle.

41 **e** All of the shapes have a line attached to an arrow. The line makes one complete, closed loop. The arrow is on the left side of the shape.

42 **e** All of the shapes are 3D.

43 **d**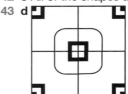

The missing square will be a diagonal reflection of the top left square.

44 **d**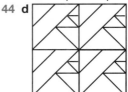

The three given squares are identical, so the missing square will look exactly the same as the others.

45 **c**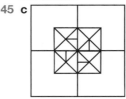

The whole shape is made from squares that are identical apart from being rotated 90° clockwise each time.

46 **b**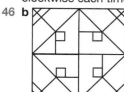

In each square, the corner design is symmetrical while the central design is rotated 90° clockwise.

47 **e**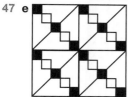

The three given squares are identical, so the missing square will look exactly the same as the others.

48 **e**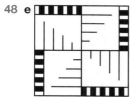

The whole shape is made from squares that are identical apart from being rotated 90° clockwise each time.

49 **c** The black and white triangles on the left of the net form the front face of the cube, the black circle forms the right face and the black and white rectangles at the top of the net form the top face.

50 **e** The top middle square with the dot forms the front face of the cube, the black and white rectangles form the right face and the bottom square with the smaller black square folds around to form the top face.

51 **c** The downward-pointing arrow one up from the bottom forms the front face of the cube, the top right arrow folds down to form the right face of the cube and the white circle forms the top face.

52 **a** The striped triangle forms the front face of the cube. The diagonal white arrow folds down to form the right face of the cube. The arrow shown on the net pointing in a north-east direction forms the top of the cube.

53 **d** The circle with the criss-cross pattern forms the front face of the cube, the circle divided into four sections folds down to form the right face and the black circle forms the top face.

54 **c** The white circle with the horizontal line forms the front face of the cube, the plain white circle forms the right face and the cross forms the top face.

55–60 When each shape is paired with the correct reflection, they form a single shape that is perfectly symmetrical.

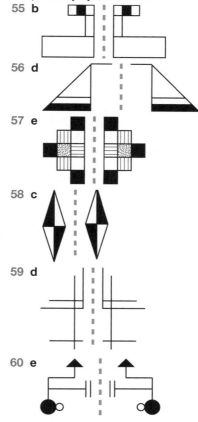

55 **b**

56 **d**

57 **e**

58 **c**

59 **d**

60 **e**

Paper 3 (pages 21–30)

1 **d** All of the long solid lines have a short solid line attached at one end, creating an 'L' shape that faces to the left or right. All shapes also have a broken line that is on the inside of the 'L' shape.

2 **e** All of the patterns are either rounded triangles in a circle, or a circle in a rounded triangle.

3 **e** All of the shapes have five sides.

4 **b** All of the shapes have two thirds in a lined pattern and one third dotted pattern.

5 **b** All of the patterns have six elements and are symmetrical. There are arranged in lines of 1, 2 and 3 shapes.

6 **a** All of the shapes are cuboids with one lined face.

7 **d** All of the patterns have a black dot in the centre. The two outer shapes are exactly the same size and shape.

8 **c** All of the shapes have five stalks.

9 **e** All of the patterns have a circle with a line running through it that then bends 90°

10 **d** All of the patterns have a circle and triangle that overlap and the section that overlaps is black.

11 **e** All of the flags have one quarter coloured black.

12 **c** All of the patterns have arrows that are the same colour as the circles.

13 **e** The pattern has one additional vertical line each time.

14 **b** The pattern has one new circle each time alternating between large and small.

15 **e** The pattern is a centre circle alternating between black and white and each time there is another ring added around the centre circle.

16 **e** The pattern has two additional stalks each time.

17 **c** The pattern has an arrow moving clockwise around the compass points from NE, E, SE, S, SW.

18 **b** The pattern has an odd number of 'pins' made from one dot and one stalk. The direction of the stalks is in an alternating pattern and two 'pins' are added each time.

19 **c** The lines at the bottom form a 'step' pattern that has one additional line each time. The vertical rectangle has a pattern of one dot with a black square above and below. This moves down one square each time.

20 **d** The pattern is black circle, two rectangles, white circle, two rectangles. The two rectangles have diagonal lines, running from bottom left to top right in the first rectangle and running from bottom right to top left in the second rectangle. The first rectangle has a shape above it and the second rectangle has the same shape below it.

21 **d** The top arrow points alternately left then right. The missing pattern has a top arrow pointing right. The black dot moves higher up the vertical line. The bottom pattern is a white rectangle that moves from left to centre to right to centre to left.

22 **d** The top of the rectangle has a gradual increase in the black and a decrease in the white. The bottom of the rectangle has a gradual increase in the white and a decrease in the black.

23 **b** The pattern alternates between two closed loops and one closed loop. The straight lines increase by one line each time.

24 **e** The pattern has five lines with a black dot on the outer lines and a small arrow at the end of the middle line. The whole group move

clockwise around the compass points from N, NE, E, SE, S.

25 **d** The first letter represents the outline (K has a thick black outline, L has a thin black outline and M has a double thin, black outline. The second letter represents the arrow lines. (X has a line without arrows on the end, Y has a line with arrows on both ends and Z has a line with one arrow on the end).

26 **c** The first letter represents the colour of the dots (A has black dots on both sides of the domino, B has white dots on both sides of the domino and C has black dots on one side and white dots on the other side). The second letter represents the equality of dots (T has the same number of dots on each side of the domino and S has a different number of dots on each side of the domino).

27 **d** The first letter represents the 3D shape (P has a cylinder, Q has a cuboid and R has a triangular prism). The second letter represents the colour of the shape (C is white and O has one face in black).

28 **c** The first letter represents the thick black line (A has a curved line and B has a straight line). The second letter represents the thin black line (R has a straight line with a white dot on the end, U has a curved line with a white square on the end, S has a curved line with a white dot at the end and T has a straight line with a white square at the end).

29 **a** The first letter represents the outline and shape (D has a double lined circle, G has a grey rounded square, E has a thick, black circle and F has a double rounded quadrilateral). The second letter represents the number of sections each shape is divided into (C has two sections, A has four sections and B has three sections).

30 **e** The first letter represents the outer flag shape (J has a rectangle, K has a wavy flag and L has a triangular flag). The second letter represents the number of sections each flag is divided into (X has three sections, Y has two sections and Z has four sections).

31 **c**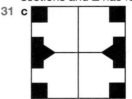

The missing square will be a vertical reflection of the bottom left square.

32 a

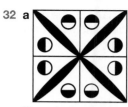

The missing square will be a vertical reflection of the bottom left square.

33 c

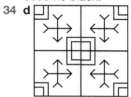

The bottom left square is the same as the top right square, but the black hoop has become white. The missing square will be the same as the top left square, but the white cross will become black.

34 d

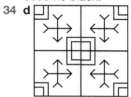

The missing square is a vertical reflection of the bottom left square.

35 e

The missing square is a 90° clockwise rotation of the top right square.

36 e

The bottom left square is the same as the top left square but the colours have reversed from white to black. The top right square will be the same as the missing bottom right square with the colours reversed from white to black.

37 a

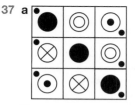

The large circle in each square has diagonal symmetry. Black dots have been added in the top left of the squares in the left column and to the bottom right of the squares in the right column. The missing square will have a black circle with a small black dot in the bottom right of the square.

38 b

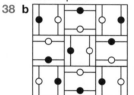

The squares on the top row are rotated 90° anticlockwise to form the middle row, and then rotated 90° anticlockwise again to form the bottom row. The missing square will therefore be the same as the middle, right square rotated 90° anticlockwise.

39 b

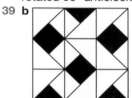

Each square is a horizontal reflection of the square above it. The missing square will therefore be a horizontal reflection of the middle right square.

40 c

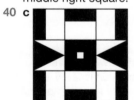

The whole square has vertical and horizontal symmetry. The missing square will therefore be a vertical reflection of the bottom left square.

Bond Non-Verbal Reasoning Assessment Papers 10–11+ years Book 1

41 d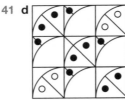

The whole square has diagonal symmetry. The missing square will be identical to the top left square.

42 e

The whole square has vertical symmetry. The missing square is a vertical reflection of the bottom left square.

43 d

The shape on the left is oriented correctly, with the bead at the right hand end. In the other shape, the horizonal lines are the right length and positioned correctly.

44 b

The flag shape is oriented correctly, with the small black squares at top left and bottom right. The large square has a thin outline on three sides, with the internal pattern unchanged.

45 e

The semi circle is white with a dividing horizontal line. It has been rotated 180°. The square has a large white area and a strip on the right divided horizontally into four small white rectangles.

46 b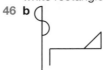

The shape on the left has two white semi circles at the top in the correct positions,

with single lines. The shape on the right has a vertical line pointing down at the left end and a right-angled triangle and the right end.

47 e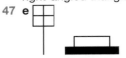

The shape on the left has two squares at the top on either side of the longer vertical line. The shape on the right has a white rectangle on top of a longer black rectangle.

48 d

The ring has an inner circle made of long dashes. The triangle is rotated 180°.

49 c In the second shape, the centre dot has become white, the wavy line has become straight and the large outer shape has a broken line inside it.

50 e In the second shape, the rectangles have become ovals, all pointing in the same directions as the rectangles.

51 c In the second shape, the shape has rotated 180°, the colours have switched places and the shape has doubled in height with the colour in the small square being stretched all the way up.

52 a In the second shape, the bottom half of the shape has been removed. At the top of the shape, the single black line has become a double black line.

53 a The second shape is a vertical reflection of the first shape.

54 c The second shape is a 90° clockwise rotation of the first shape. In the second shape, the grid pattern has become white and the shape with vertical stripes has become black.

55 d The second shape is a 90° anticlockwise rotation of the first shape. In the second shape, the circles has become larger and the squares have become smaller. The white circles have become black.

56 d The first shape has a central 'pole' with lines protruding from each side. The lines on the left hand side of the pole stay the same, whereas the lines on the right hand side are flipped over horizontally.

57 e The second shape is a vertical reflection of the first shape. In the second shape, the white circle has become black, and the thick line has become thinner.

58 d In the second shape, the straight lines at the top have become waved lines, and the circles/ovals have become squares/rectangles. The wavy pattern has become black, and the black has become a wavy pattern.

59 b In the second shape, the thin lines have become thick and the thick line has become thin.

60 c The second shape is a vertical reflection of the first shape. In the second shape, the white squares have become black and the black circles have become white.

Paper 4 (pages 31–40)

1 e All of the shapes are squares with a smaller shape that fits totally inside.

2 c All of the shapes have a double lined outline.

3 b All of the patterns have a line that begins inside the shape and ends outside of the shape. It only crosses the outside of the shape once.

4 c All of the patterns are made from two triangles with a circle inside the largest triangle.

5 d All of the patterns have a background shape with a black square in front of it.

6 d All of the shapes have two right angles with one or two thick black lines.

7 d All of the shapes have one solid line and one dashed line.

8 c All of the flags are divided into four sections. Two sections are white, one is black and one has diagonal line.

9 e All of the shapes are cylinders with a straight line bisecting one face.

10 a All of the shapes have one thick, black line and one thick, white line. The lines follow each other and both ends of both lines are level.

11 e All of the circles have a small black area with a black circle on the outside to the side of the black area.

12 b All of the patterns have a black circle with three sticks of the same design coming from it.

13 c The top white rectangle moves down each time, but remains the same length. The bottom black rectangle moves down each time, but remains the same length. The middle horizontal line moves down and gets longer each time.

14 d Each square on the grid moves one place to the right each time. The square to the left of a black square always has a dot.

15 b The sequence has an increasing number of loops.

16 c The angle between the vertical line and the line with the small arrow head increases by the same amount each time. The arrow head is always an open V.

17 b The shapes alternate between a small square and a large square. The small squares alternate between a black circle in a white square and a white circle in a black square.

18 a The top black shape decreases in size. The number of horizontal lines increases by one each time.

19 e Each shape consists of two large squares on top of each other. The shapes swap places so that the large square with this four triangles is alternately on the top and on the bottom. When the large square with the four triangles is on top, the black dot is in the bottom triangle and the striped triangle is on the left. In the other large square, the number of black squares increases.

20 a The number of small rectangles alternates between one and two. The number of dots in the small rectangles increases each time there is a shape with one small rectangle. The colour of the dots alternates between black and white. The black stripe in the larger, bottom rectangle moves to the right.

21 b The shapes increase by a horizontal line or a black rectangle, alternately.

22 e The shapes alternate between a circle and a square. The squares are alternately divided into four squares and into four triangles. The triangles within the squares are black and white, and this pattern rotates clockwise.

23 d Each shape has one fewer sides than the previous shape. The pattern in the shapes follows the sequence black, diagonal lines, grid.

24 e The number of wavy lines at the top increases. The circles alternate between white and black. In the rectangle at the bottom, the black square and square with the dot move across each row one square at a time, from left to right.

25–30 When each shape is paired with the correct reflection, they form a single shape that is perfectly symmetrical.

25 b

26 e

27 e

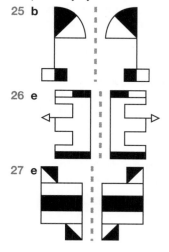

EXPANDED ANSWERS

Bond Non-Verbal Reasoning Assessment Papers 10–11+ years Book 1

28 **c**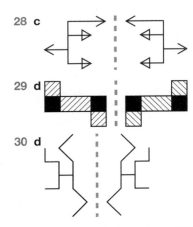

29 **d**

30 **d**

31 **d** The second shape is a 180° rotation of the first shape. The black shapes have become white.

32 **c** The second shape is a vertical reflection of the first shape. The colours have been reversed.

33 **a** In the second shape, the colours have been reversed.

34 **d** In the second shape, the straight lines have become wavy and the wavy lines have become straight.

35 **c** In the second shape, each stripe has become a circle.

36 **d** The second shape is a vertical reflection of the first shape. The arrow heads have become black dots.

37 **a** In the second shape, the dotted lines have become diagonal lines, from top left to bottom right. The diagonal lines have become dotted lines.

38 **d** In the first pair the two triangles have become circles and the circle has become a triangle. They have swapped shapes. Therefore, in the second pair the two squares will become triangles and the triangle will become a square.

39 **d** In the second shape, the overall shape should match the first shape. Then the sequence of line style should mirror that of the first shape, though may be in a different order – solid, solid, dash, dash-dot-dash.

40 **e** In the second shape, all the windows from the first shape are packed tightly in a diagonal line.

41 **b** In the second pattern, each large circle has become two small circles. The black circles have become white and the white circles have become black.

42 **e** The second shape is the first shape rotated by 90°, 180° and 270° clockwise.

43 **d**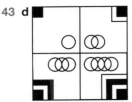

A white outline, then a black outline is added to the square in each corner as it moves in a clockwise direction. A circle is added, moving along each row of squares from left to right. The top left square has 1 circle, the top right square has 2 circles, the bottom left has 3 circles and the bottom right has 4 circles.

44 **d**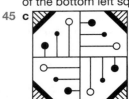

The missing square will be a vertical reflection of the bottom left square.

45 **c**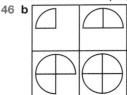

The missing square will be a 90° clockwise rotation of the top right square.

46 **b**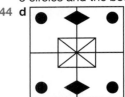

A quarter of the circle is added each time, moving along each row of squares from left to right. The top left square has one quarter of a circle, the top right has two quarters of a circle, the bottom left has three quarters of a circle and the bottom right has four quarters.

47 **e**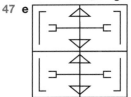

The missing square will be a vertical reflection of the bottom left square.

48 e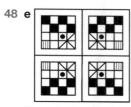

The missing square will be a vertical reflection of the bottom left square.

49 a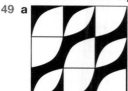

Each row of the square has the same three squares in the same order. The missing square will be the same as the top left square and the middle square.

50 d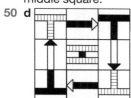

Each outer square is a 180° rotation of its opposite square. The missing square will therefore be a 180° rotation of the top middle square.

51 c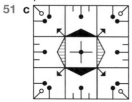

The missing square will be a vertical reflection of the bottom left square.

52 a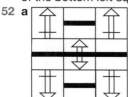

The missing square will be a vertical reflection of the bottom left square.

53 c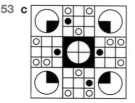

The missing square will be a 180° rotation of the top middle square.

54 d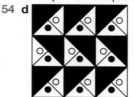

In each row, the three squares are the same. The missing square will be the same as the middle left and centre squares.

55 d The arrow forms the front face of the cube, the black and white stripes at the top of the net form the right face and the black and white stripes in the centre of the net form the top face.

56 e The black strip forms the front face, the arrow forms the right face and the X forms the top face.

57 d The arrow forms the front face, the cross with the black triangle forms the right face and the black cross forms the top face.

58 c The white and striped rectangles form the front face, the three dots form the right face and the white circle on the right of the net forms the top face.

59 e The white circle form the front face, the arrow that points to the left in the net forms the right face and the gridded shape forms the top face.

60 d The arrow with the closed arrow head forms the top face, the arrow at the bottom right of the net forms the right face and the plus sign forms the top face.

Paper 5 (pages 41–50)

1 c The black segment rotates clockwise around the circle, 45° each time.

2 d The number of squares at the top increases by one each time. The first block nearest the vertical line is alternately black and white, and the following squares also alternate between black and white. The number of horizontal lines at the bottom increases by one each time and they zigzag up the vertical line.

3 **e** The sequence is a reflection with the mirror line in the centre of the middle block.

4 **a** This is a repeating sequence, with the first two blocks repeated alternately.

5 **c** The top row is a repeating pattern of circle, grey square, triangle. The bottom row is a repeating pattern of triangle, square, circle, square.

6 **b** The number of rows of small squares increases by one each time. In each row, the black and white blocks alternate.

7 **d** The number of short horizontal lines at the bottom increases by one each time. The short horizontal line on the right moves up the long vertical line.

8 **e** Working from the bottom, one black dot is replaced by a white dot each time.

9 **d** Working from the bottom right, one black dot is removed each time. The number of crosses decreases by one each time, and these move across to the right.

10 **c** The central arrow points alternately to top right and to bottom right. The circles are alternately both black, and white and white with a dot.

11 **c** The shaded sectors all rotate clockwise around the circle, one sector at a time.

12 **a** One shape is removed from the top of the pattern each time.

13 **b** The second shape fits into the 'gap' in the first shape to form a quadrilateral. The direction of the lines in the second shape has been changed.

14 **c** The second shape is a vertical reflection of the first shape.

15 **e** In the second shape, the wavy line has become straight and overlaps the shapes. The circles have also become squares.

16 **b** The second shape is a 90° clockwise rotation of the first shape. In the second shape, the black squares have become white squares with crosses, and the white squares with crosses have become black squares.

17 **e** In the second shape, the overlapping shapes from the first shape have been moved apart, shrunk in size and been placed above and below the black central shape. The black central shape has been formed from where the larger shapes have overlapped.

18 **e** In the second shape, circles have been placed over the central stems. The number of circles is the same as the number of stems in the first shape.

19 **c** In the second pattern, the top shape has been moved down and the bottom shape has been moved up so both outer shapes are inside the middle shape.

20 **c** The second shape is a vertical reflection of the first shape.

21 **d** The second shape is a vertical reflection of the first shape. In the second shape, the thin lines become thick and the thick lines become thin.

22 **d** The second shape is a vertical reflection of the first shape.

23 **b** The second shape is a 180° rotation of the first shape.

24 **c** In the second shape, the dots and black squares have swapped places. The lined and white squares have also swapped places.

25 **a** The first letter represents the pattern of the inside shape (A has white, B has diagonal stripes and C has black). The second letter represents the pattern of the outer shape (A has white, B has diagonal stripes and C has black).

26 **a** The first letter represents the proportion of the shape that is black (X has half the shape black, Y has one third of the shape black and Z has one quarter of the shape black). The second letter represents the shape (A has a circle, B has a square and C has a triangle).

27 **e** The first letter represents the type of arrow head (S has a closed black arrow head, T has an open arrow head and U has a closed white arrow head). The second letter represents the stem of the arrow (M has a dotted line pattern, N has a single, thin line and O has a thick white line).

28 **b** The first letter represents the top shape and colour (A has a white circle, B has a black circle, C has a black square and D has a white square). The second letter represents the bottom cross (Y has a diagonal cross, X has no cross and Z has a 'plus' cross).

29 **b** The first letter represents the outside shape (R has a square, S has a triangle and T has a circle). The second letter represents the inside shape (X has a circle, Y has a square and Z has a triangle).

30 **d** The first letter represents the vertical line (H has a thick black line, J has a thick white line and K has a thick dotted line). The second letter represents the shape that goes with the lines (C has a black triangle, B has a white rectangle and A has a circle).

31 **e** All of the patterns have a black square.

32 **d** All of the patterns have a white circle, a straight line and a black triangle.

33 **d** All of the patterns have a stick that begins outside of the shape and then touches two outside edges of the shape without crossing over the shape.

34 **c** All of the patterns have three elements with the middle one black.

35 **d** All of the shapes are rectangles with one arrow that crosses the rectangle and one stick

with a reverse arrow head that also crosses the rectangle. The arrow head and reverse arrow head need to be pointing in the same direction.

36 **a** All of the patterns have two small triangles and one small circle and all three shapes have different shading.

37 **c** All of the shapes have one central line with two symmetrical lines that cross over it.

38 **e** All of the grids have three black squares; two on the edges of the grid and one in the central area of the grid.

39 **e** All of the shapes are circles divided equally in two. One half of each circle is white and the other half is lined.

40 **e** All of the patterns have one white circle at one end of a right-angled line. A second line is perpendicular to this line.

41 **e** All of the shapes are arches. The outline of the arch is the same design as the central pair of parallel lines.

42 **c** All of the shapes are four-sided with a circle inside the shape. The two patterns in all of the shapes are black and striped.

43 **a**

The missing square will be a vertical reflection of the bottom left square.

44 **e**

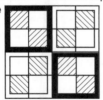

The missing square will be a diagonal reflection of the top left square.

45 **e**

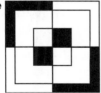

The missing square will be a diagonal reflection of the top left square.

46 **d**

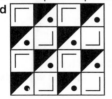

The three given squares are identical, so the missing square will look exactly the same as the others.

47 **a**

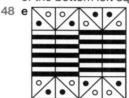

The missing square will be a vertical reflection of the bottom left square.

48 **e**

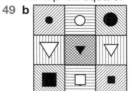

The missing square will be a 180° rotation of the top left square.

49 **b**

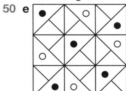

Each row has a small, medium and large version of a particular shape. The shapes alternate between black and white, along each row. In each column, the background shading has horizontal symmetry. The missing shape will therefore be a medium sized, white square on a background of horizontal stripes.

50 **e**

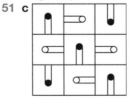

The missing square will match the top left and middle square as the pattern is repeating diagonally.

51 **c**

Working from left to right, the circles have lines pointing down, left, up, right. The circles are alternately black and white. The missing square will therefore have a black circle with lines pointing down.

52 e

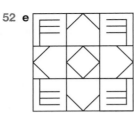

The missing square will be vertical reflection of the bottom left square.

53 d

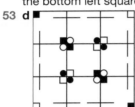

The missing square will be a diagonal reflection of the top left square.

54 e

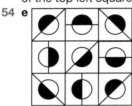

Working from left to right, the pattern in each square rotates clockwise. The missing square will have a horizontal line, with the black half of the circle at the bottom.

55 c

56 e

57 d

58 d

59 d

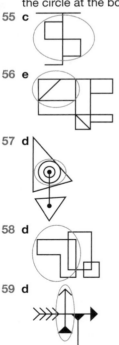

60 b

Paper 6 (pages 51–60)

1 **b** All of the shapes apart from b have a shorter horizontal line above the longer horizontal line.

2 **c** All of the shapes apart from c have vertical and horizontal symmetry and have been divided into equal sections.

3 **d** All of the circles apart from d have a black dot on the outer edge.

4 **d** All of the patterns apart from d have a tick.

5 **c** All of the shapes apart from c have at least one diagonal line.

6 **d** All of the shapes apart from d have the same number of elements in both halves of the shape.

7 **b** A circle or arrow is added alternately to the bottom of each pattern. The styles of the arrow heads stay the same each time in each part of the sequence.

8 **a** Each pattern has one more line, and one more cross, than the previous pattern.

9 **a** A new line is added each time, crossing the previous line and creating a new black area.

10 **b** A new circle is added each time. The colour of the circles alternates between all white and all black.

11 **c** A short horizontal line is added at the top each time and a short horizontal line is removed at the bottom each time.

12 **e** A new shape is added inside the previous shapes each time.

13 **c** All of the patterns are triangles with a circle that touches the triangle but does not overlap it.

14 **d** All of the shapes are right angles with both 'arms' the same length and width.

15 **e** All of the patterns form an 'S' shape, not a backwards 'S' shape.

16 **c** All of the patterns have two identical triangles forming a bow shape, with a different shape at the centre.

17 **b** All of the patterns have a triangle hovering above a rectangle of the same length.

18 **c** All of the patterns have a small version of the same shape inside them.

19 **d** All of the flags are half black and half white.

20 **e** All of the patterns have the square and stem in the same colour and the circle in a different colour.

21 **d** All of the patterns consist of a thick, black line, plus two thin, black lines.

22 **b** All of the shapes are squares with one black corner.

23 d All of the shapes have one arch section taken out of the shape. All of the other sides are straight.

24 b In all of the shapes, the lines cross at four points.

25–30 When each shape is paired with the correct reflection, they form a single shape that is perfectly symmetrical.

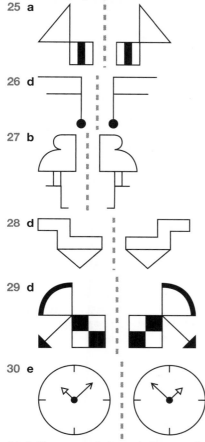

25 a

26 d

27 b

28 d

29 d

30 e

31 b The second shape is a copy of the first shape with a horizontal reflection of the first shape.

32 c The second shape is a 90° anticlockwise copy of the first shape. A vertical reflection of the shape, after it has been rotated, has been added to it.

33 d The second shape is the left hand line from the first shape.

34 c The second shape is a 180° rotation of the first shape. In the first pair, the top shape stays black and the bottom shape stays white. The second pair will follow the same pattern.

35 c In the second shape, the small black rectangle has become a large white rectangle. The short lines have been made the same length to form small rectangles at the end of the larger rectangle.

36 d The second shape is the first shape rotated 180°. In the second shape white has become black and circles have become squares.

37 a The second shapes is the first shape rotated 90° clockwise. In the second shape, black has become white and white has become black.

38 b The second shape is a vertical reflection of the first shape.

39 e In the second shape, squares have become circles and circles have become squares.

40 a Joined together, the first shape and second shape make a rectangle.

41 e In the second shape, the inner outline is dashed. The shading in the inner shape has become black.

42 e In the second shape, the right-angled stalks have become curved, in the same direction as in the first shape. The central black square has become a circle.

43 b The cross and the white circle are in opposite positions, so they cannot therefore be seen as adjacent faces on the cube.

44 d When the black circle forms the front face of the cube, the arrow on the top will point towards it.

45 e Two of the faces with grey triangles are in opposite positions, so all three cannot therefore be seen as adjacent faces on the cube.

46 c The horizontal arrow points to a grey section of one of the faces with two grey triangles.

47 a When the single dot forms the right face of the cube, the two dots on the top will run from front left to back right.

48 e When the three black dots form the front face and top face, the right face should be the side with white dots and one black dot running horizontally. In e it shows the right side as having two black dots and one white dot.

49 e

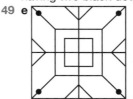

The missing square will be a vertical reflection of the bottom left square.

50 d

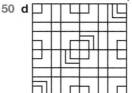

The missing square will be a diagonal reflection of the top left square.

51 e

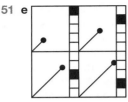

Working from left to right, the black square moves down one each time and the line with the dot becomes longer.

52 e

The missing square will be a horizontal reflection of the top right square, with colour changing from white to black.

53 c

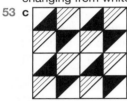

All the squares are identical so the missing square will be the same as the others.

54 c

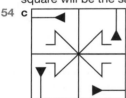

Within the missing square, the line with the triangle on the end will be 90° clockwise rotation of the line and triangle in the top right square. The zigzag line will be a vertical reflection of the zigzag line in the bottom left square.

55 e

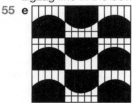

The missing square will be a vertical reflection of the bottom left square.

56 d

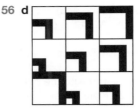

The missing square will be a diagonal reflection of the top left square.

57 d

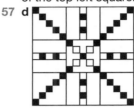

The missing square will be a vertical reflection of the bottom left square.

58 d

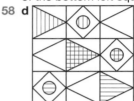

Each row has a triangle pointing left, a triangle pointing right and a square with a circle in it. The triangle pointing right and the circle have the same shading. The missing square will therefore have a triangle pointing right, with horizontal lines.

59 b

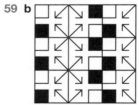

The missing square will be a vertical reflection of the bottom middle square, with the colour of the squares swapped.

60 a

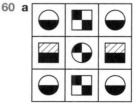

The four corner squares are identical so the missing square will be the same as the other three corners.

Paper 4

Which shape on the right goes best with the shapes on the left? Circle the letter.

Example

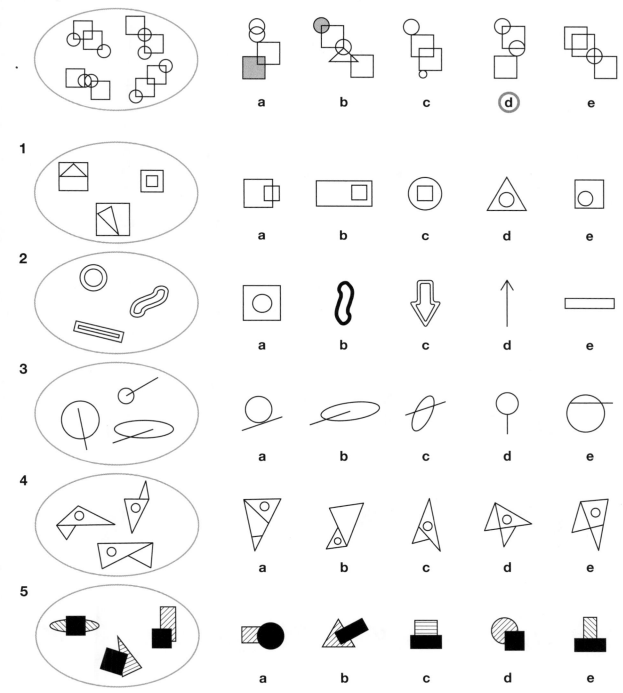

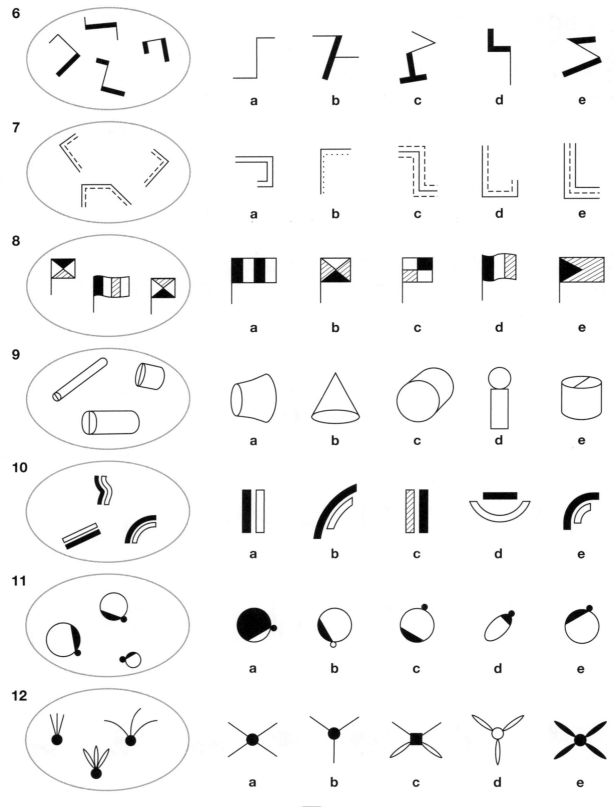

Which one comes next? Circle the letter.

Example

　?　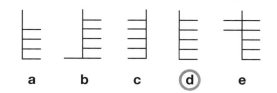

a　　b　　c　　(d)　　e

13　　?　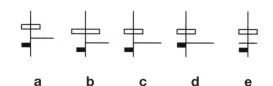

a　　b　　c　　d　　e

14　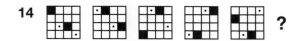　?　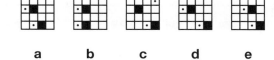

a　　b　　c　　d　　e

15　　?　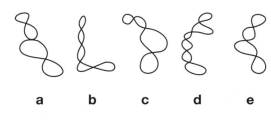

a　　b　　c　　d　　e

16　　?　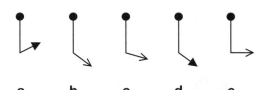

a　　b　　c　　d　　e

17　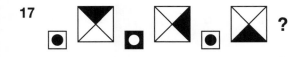　?　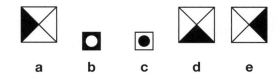

a　　b　　c　　d　　e

18　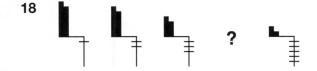　?　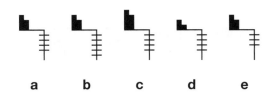

a　　b　　c　　d　　e

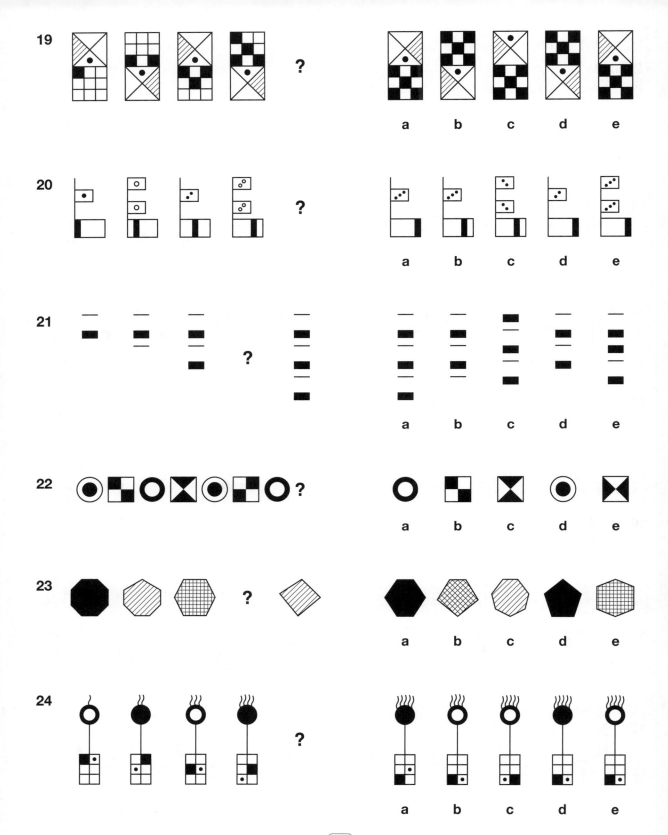

19

a　　b　　c　　d　　e

20

a　　b　　c　　d　　e

21

?

a　　b　　c　　d　　e

22

?

a　　b　　c　　d　　e

23

?

a　　b　　c　　d　　e

24

?

a　　b　　c　　d　　e

34

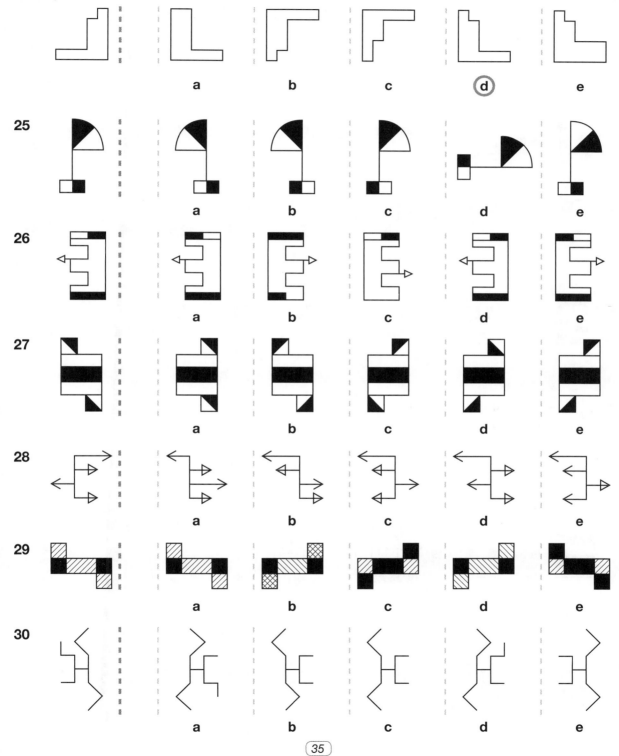

B 7 Which shape on the right is the reflection of the shape given on the left?
Circle the letter.

Example

| a | b | c | d | e |

25

| a | b | c | d | e |

26

| a | b | c | d | e |

27

| a | b | c | d | e |

28

| a | b | c | d | e |

29

| a | b | c | d | e |

30

| a | b | c | d | e |

Which shape or pattern on the right completes the second pair in the same way as the first pair? Circle the letter.

Example

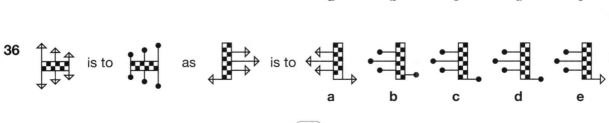

31

32

33

34

35

36

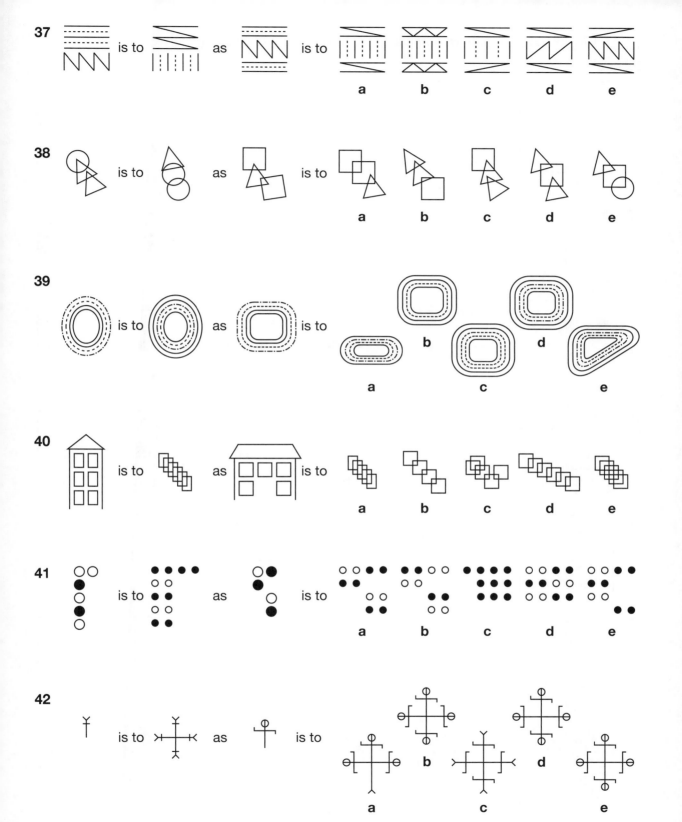

37

38

39

40

41

42

Which shape or pattern completes the larger square? Circle the letter.

Example

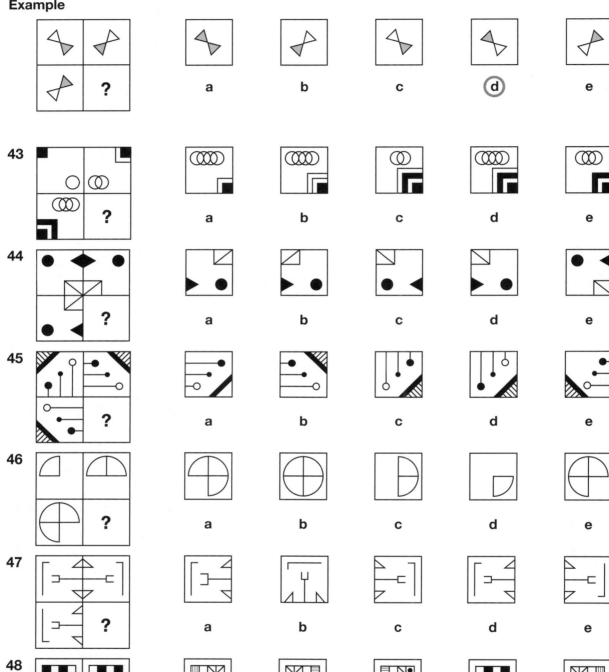

43

44

45

46

47

48

a b c d e

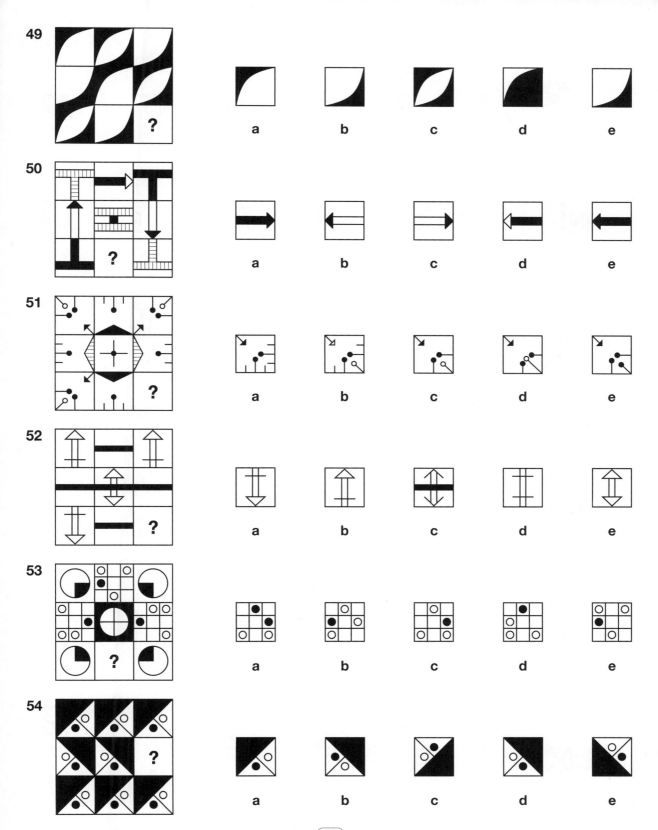

Which cube can be made from the given net? Circle the letter.

Example

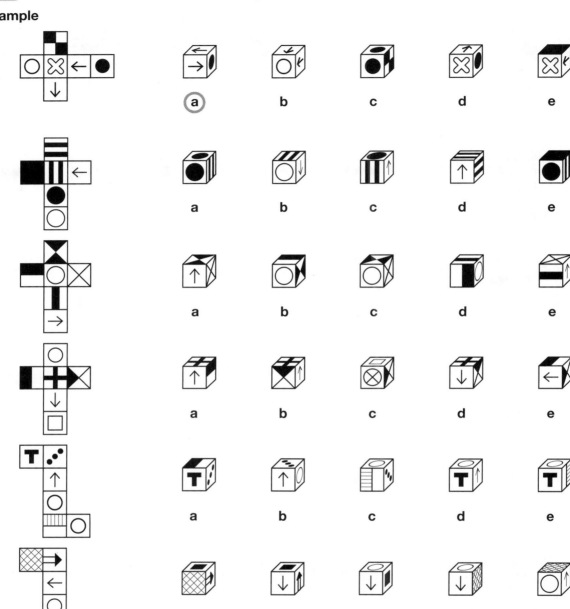

55

56

57

58

59

60

Paper 5

B 4 Which one comes next? Circle the letter.

Example

 ?

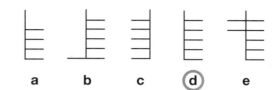

a   b   c   (d)   e

1
 ?

a   b   c   d   e

2
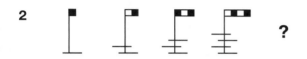 ?

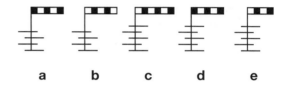

a   b   c   d   e

3
 ?

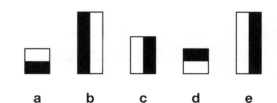

a   b   c   d   e

4
 ?

a   b   c   d   e

5
 ?

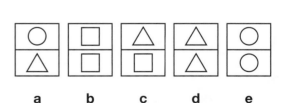

a   b   c   d   e

6
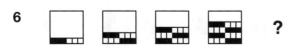 ?

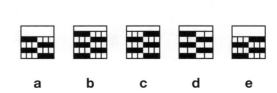

a   b   c   d   e

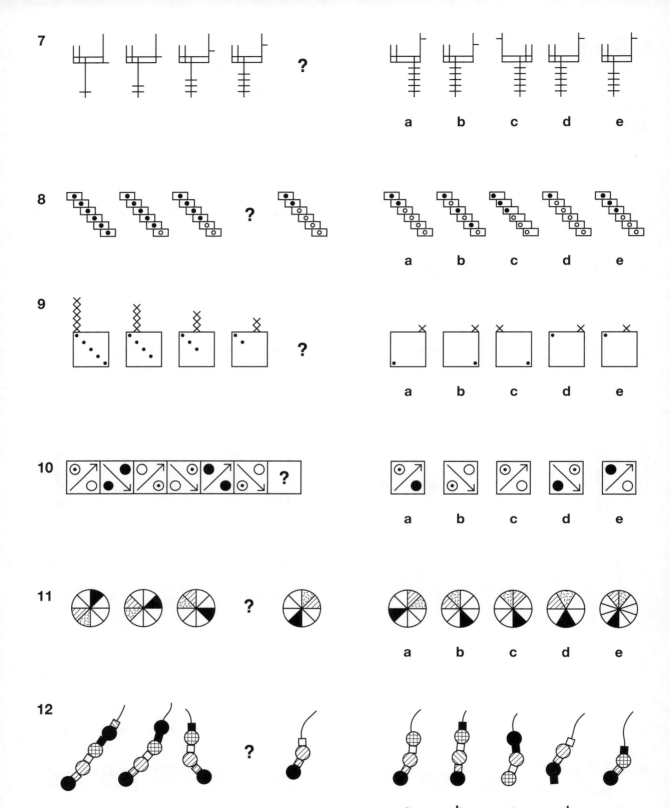

Which shape or pattern on the right completes the second pair in the same way as the first pair? Circle the letter.

Example

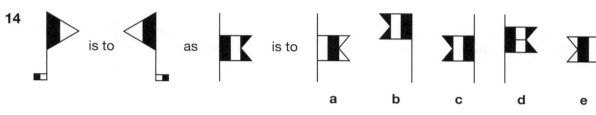

13

14

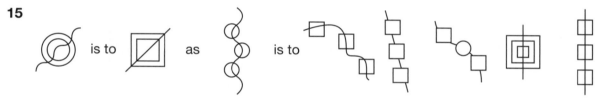

15

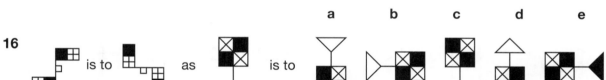

16

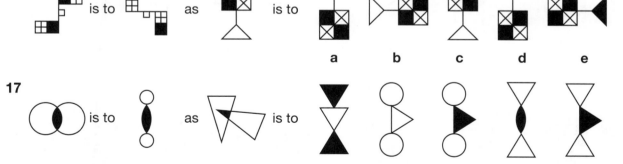

17

18

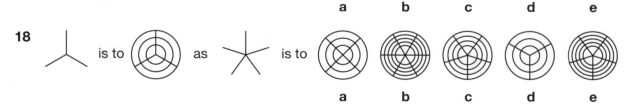

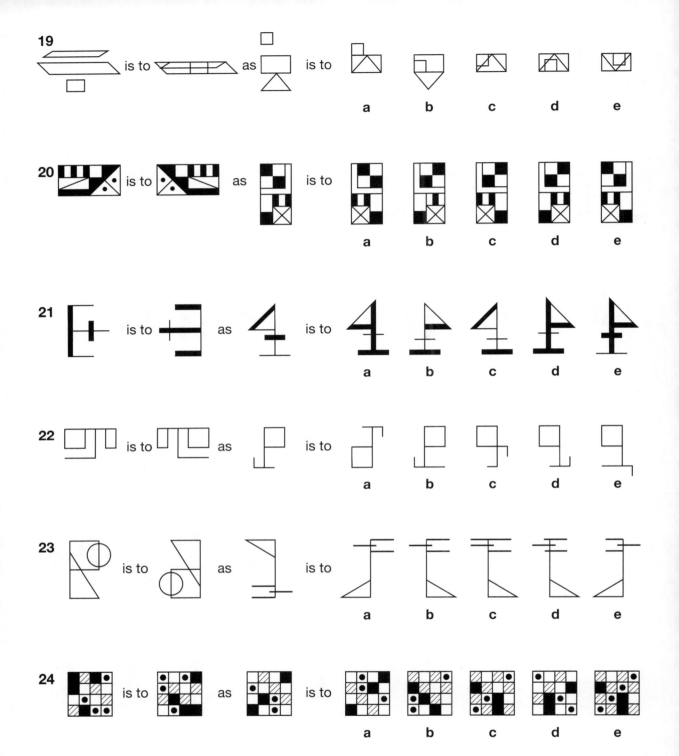

19   is to   as   is to

a   b   c   d   e

20   is to   as   is to

a   b   c   d   e

21   is to   as   is to

a   b   c   d   e

22   is to   as   is to

a   b   c   d   e

23   is to   as   is to

a   b   c   d   e

24   is to   as   is to

a   b   c   d   e

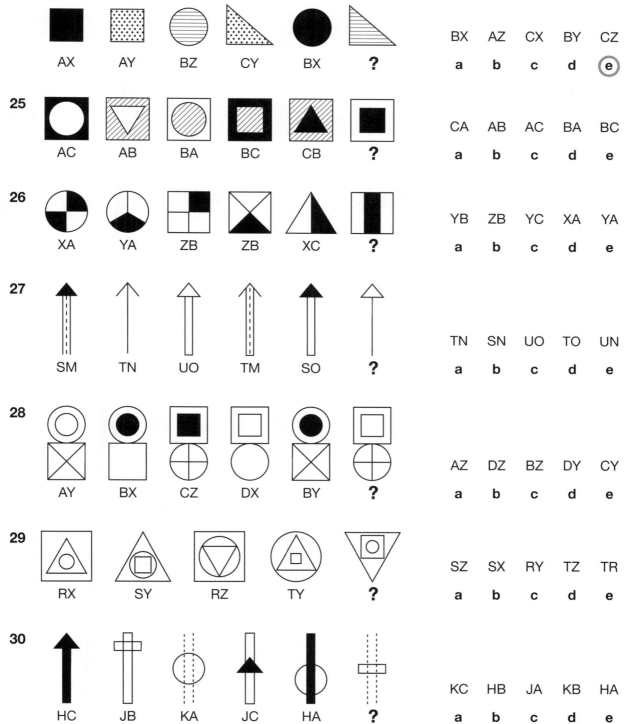

B 9 Which code matches the shape or pattern given at the end of each line?
Circle the letter.

Example

						BX	AZ	CX	BY	CZ
AX	AY	BZ	CY	BX	?	a	b	c	d	(e)

25

						CA	AB	AC	BA	BC
AC	AB	BA	BC	CB	?	a	b	c	d	e

26

						YB	ZB	YC	XA	YA
XA	YA	ZB	ZB	XC	?	a	b	c	d	e

27

						TN	SN	UO	TO	UN
SM	TN	UO	TM	SO	?	a	b	c	d	e

28

						AZ	DZ	BZ	DY	CY
AY	BX	CZ	DX	BY	?	a	b	c	d	e

29

						SZ	SX	RY	TZ	TR
RX	SY	RZ	TY	?	a	b	c	d	e

30

						KC	HB	JA	KB	HA
HC	JB	KA	JC	HA	?	a	b	c	d	e

45

B 2 Which shape on the right goes best with the shapes on the left? Circle the letter.

Example

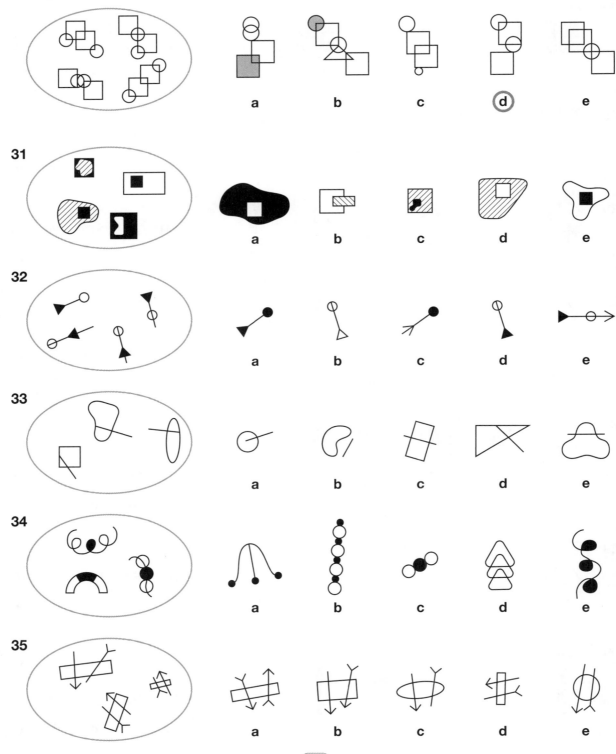

a b c (d) e

31

a b c d e

32

a b c d e

33

a b c d e

34

a b c d e

35

a b c d e

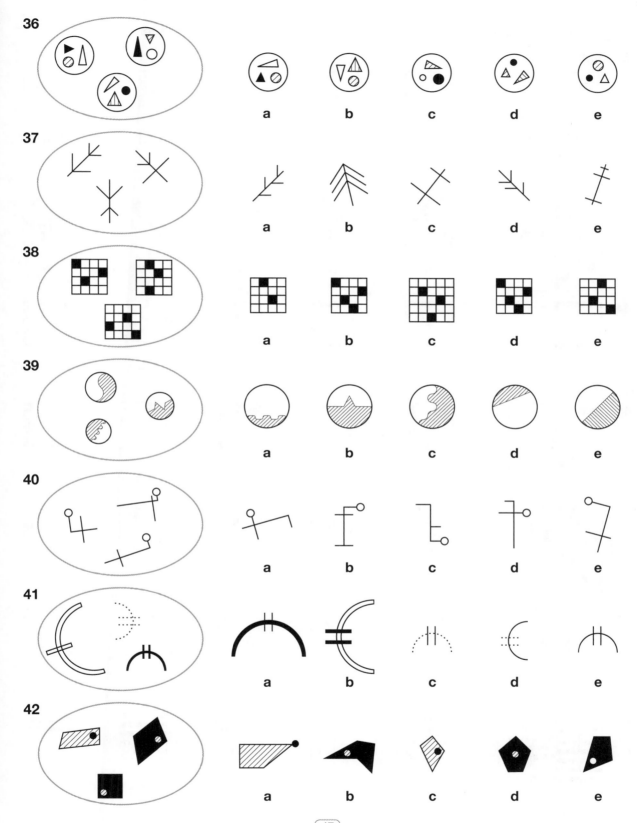

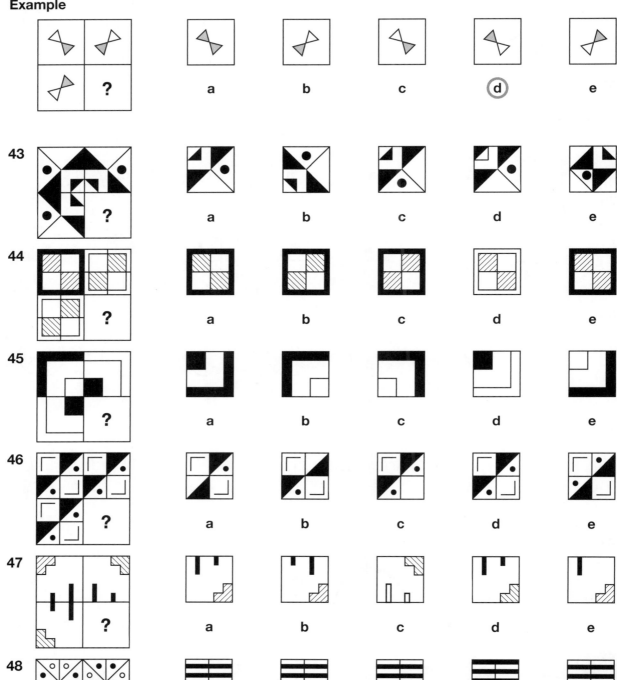

B 6 Which shape or pattern completes the larger square? Circle the letter.

Example

43

44

45

46

47

48

a   b   c   d   e

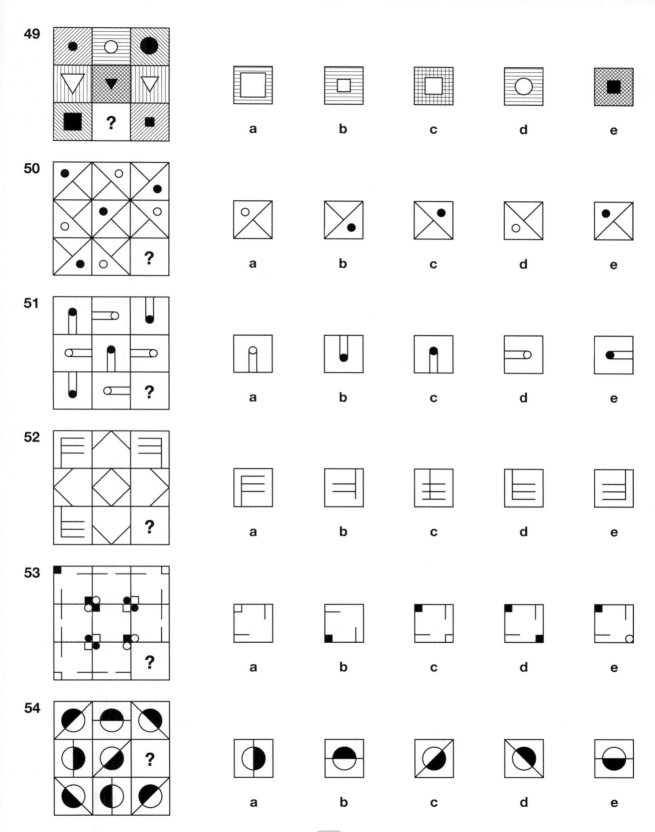

49

50

51

52

53

54

a   b   c   d   e

B 5 In which larger shape is the shape on the left hidden? Circle the letter.

Example

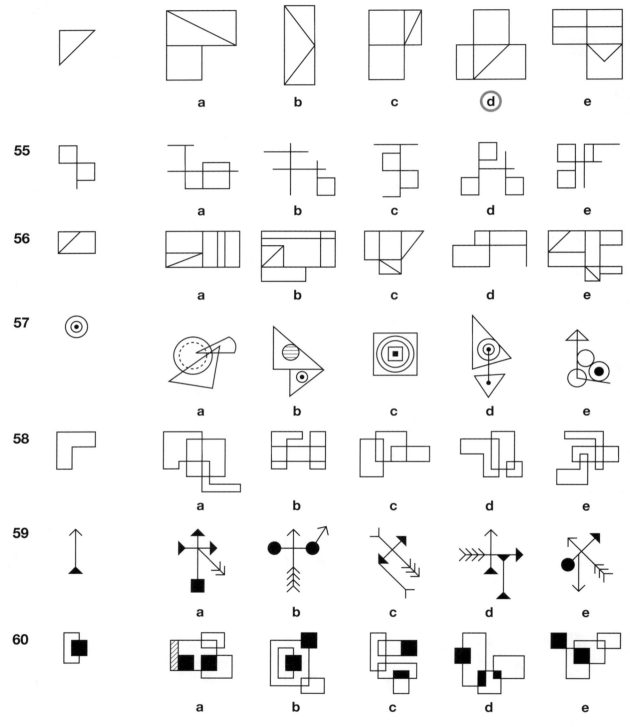

a   b   c   d   e

55

56

57

58

59

60

Paper 6

B 1 Which is the odd one out? Circle the letter.

Example

a　　　　　b　　　　　Ⓒ　　　　　d　　　　　e

1

a　　　　　b　　　　　c　　　　　d　　　　　e

2

a　　　　　b　　　　　c　　　　　d　　　　　e

3

a　　　　　b　　　　　c　　　　　d　　　　　e

4

a　　　　　b　　　　　c　　　　　d　　　　　e

5

a　　　　　b　　　　　c　　　　　d　　　　　e

6

a　　　　　b　　　　　c　　　　　d　　　　　e

Which one comes next? Circle the letter.

Example

a   b   c   (d)   e

7

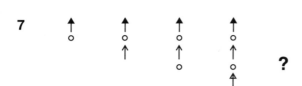

a   b   c   d   e

8

a   b   c   d   e

9

a   b   c   d   e

10

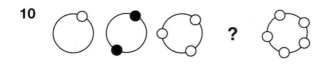

a   b   c   d   e

11

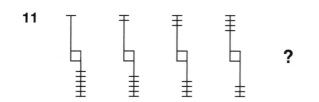

a   b   c   d   e

12

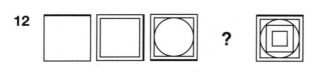

a   b   c   d   e

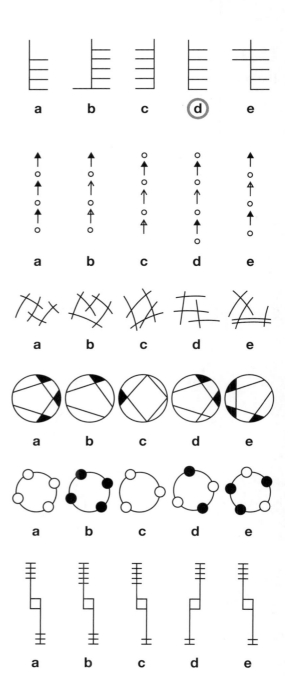

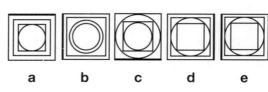

B 2 Which shape on the right goes best with the shapes on the left? Circle the letter.

Example

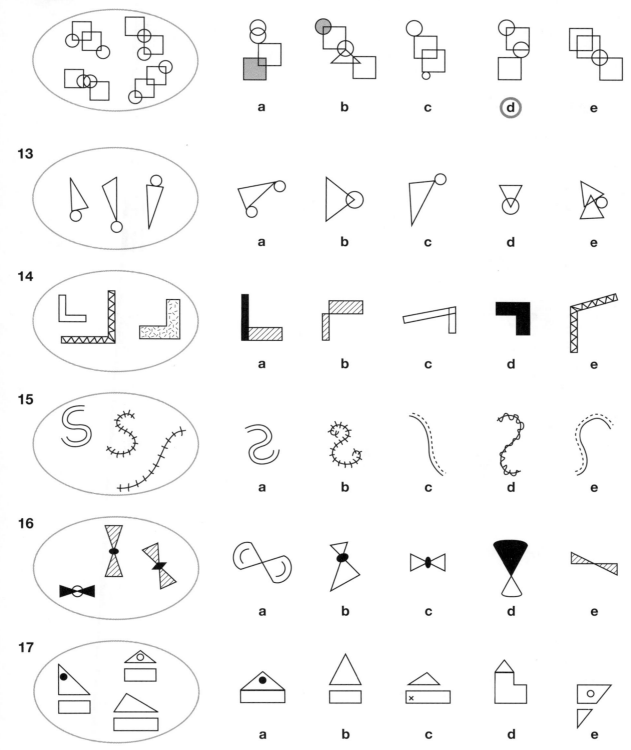

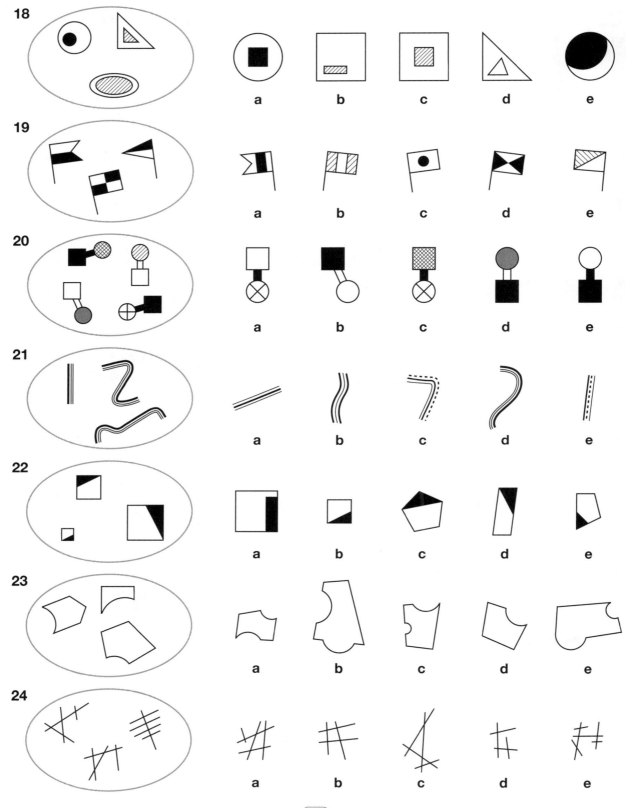

18

a   b   c   d   e

19

a   b   c   d   e

20

a   b   c   d   e

21

a   b   c   d   e

22

a   b   c   d   e

23

a   b   c   d   e

24

a   b   c   d   e

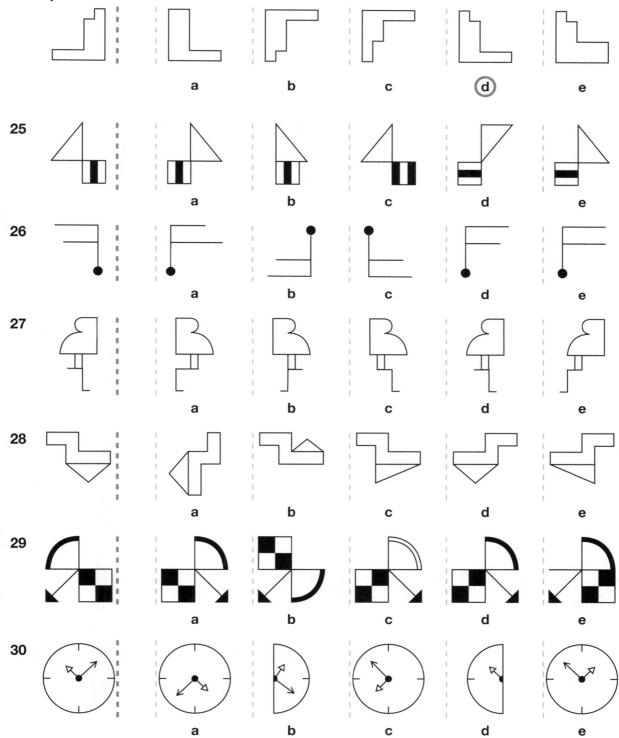

B 7 Which shape on the right is the reflection of the shape given on the left? Circle the letter.

Example

a   b   c   (d)   e

25

a   b   c   d   e

26

a   b   c   d   e

27

a   b   c   d   e

28

a   b   c   d   e

29

a   b   c   d   e

30

a   b   c   d   e

B3 Which shape or pattern on the right completes the second pair in the same way as the first pair? Circle the letter.

Example

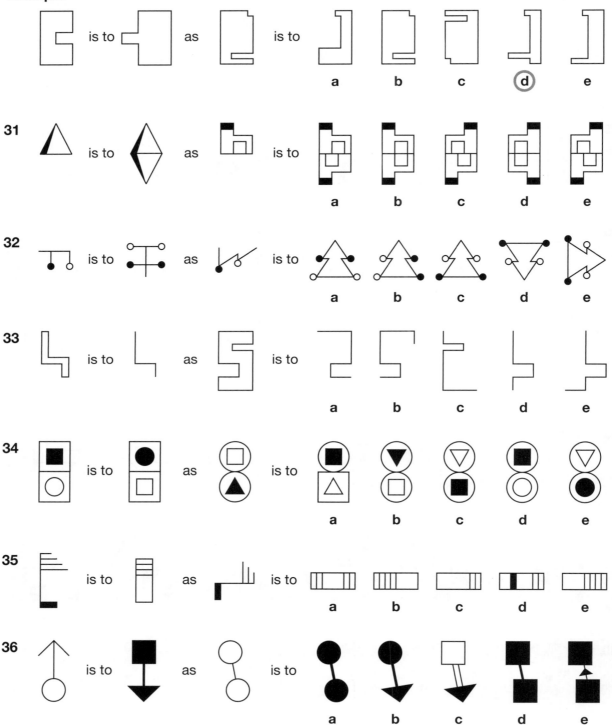

31

32

33

34

35

36

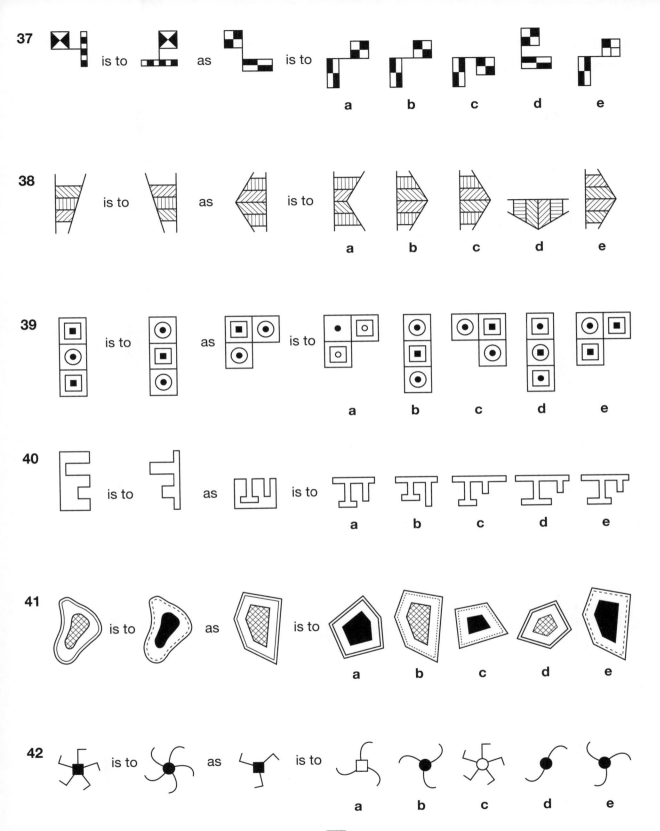

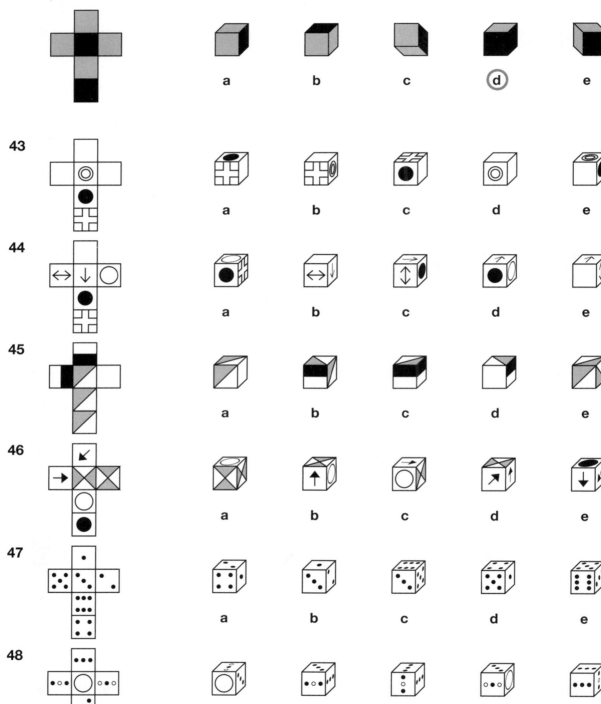

B 8 Which cube cannot be made from the given net? Circle the letter.

Example

a　　　b　　　c　　　d　　　e

43　　　　a　　　b　　　c　　　d　　　e

44　　　　a　　　b　　　c　　　d　　　e

45　　　　a　　　b　　　c　　　d　　　e

46　　　　a　　　b　　　c　　　d　　　e

47　　　　a　　　b　　　c　　　d　　　e

48　　　　a　　　b　　　c　　　d　　　e

Which shape or pattern completes the larger square? Circle the letter.

Example

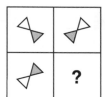

a

b

c

(d)

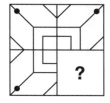
e

49

a

b

c

d

e

50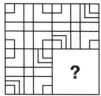

a

b

c

d

e

51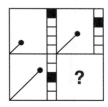

a

b

c

d

e

52

a

b

c

d

e

53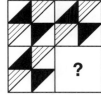

a

b

c

d

e

54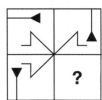

a

b

c

d

e

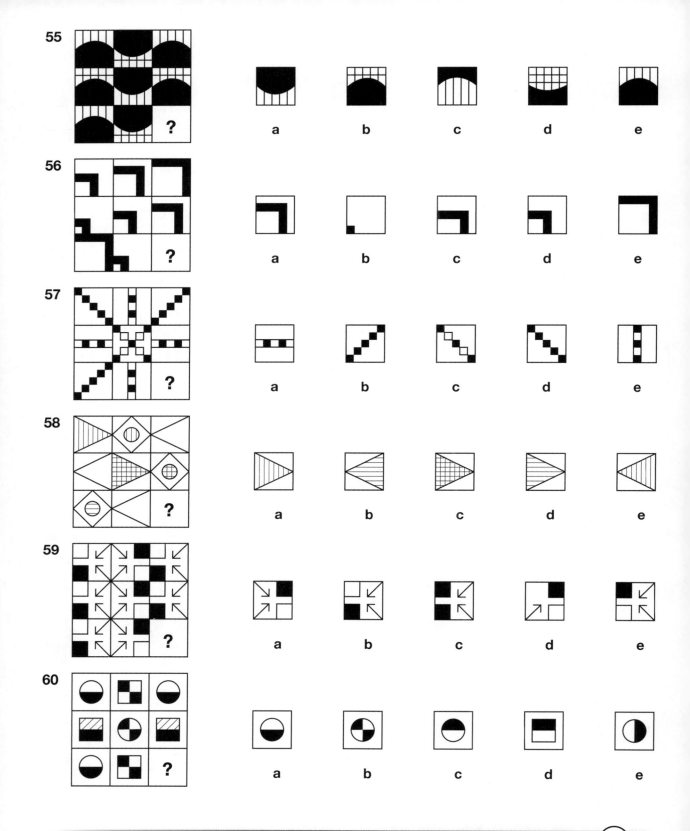

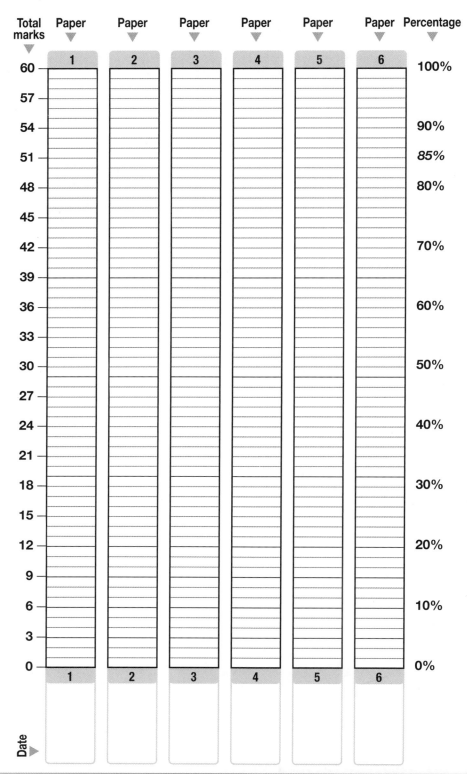